WHEN ALL SEEMS LOST,
THERE ARE...

Prayers

for

TROUBLED
TIMES

Contributors

Jeannie St. John Taylor (General Editor & contributor)
Brian Burdon
Sandy Cathcart
Marilyn Dale
Terri Eastburn
Tom Fuller
Judy Gann
Helen Haidle
Amy Haskins
Mike Haskins
Kathi Kingma
Dixie Lynn Johnson
Barbara Martin
Bette Nordberg
Cherie Norman
Ginni Poulous
Petey Prater
Betty Ritchie
Nancy Russell
Sharon Smith
Susan Standley
Ray Taylor
Ron Taylor
Ty Taylor
Glenn Thomas

Prayers

for
TROUBLED
TIMES

Jeannie St. John Taylor

AMG *Publishers*

Prayers for Troubled Times

Copyright © 2002 by Jeannie St. John Taylor
Published by AMG Publishers
6815 Shallowford Rd.
Chattanooga, Tennessee 37421

ISBN 0-89957-392-4

Cover designed by Phillip Rodgers, AMG Publishers

Edited by Mary McNeil and Tricia Toney

Interior Design and Typesetting by Reider Publishing Services, San Francisco, California

Printed in the United States of American
08 07 06 05 04 03 02 –R– 8 7 6 5 4 3 2 1

Dedication

We dedicate this book to the One True God
And to His only begotten Son, Jesus,
In whose name we offer every prayer in these pages.

Contents

SECTION ONE

Praying for Myself

. . . on endings

SECTION TWO
Praying for Others

. . . for children

SECTION THREE

Praying Together

Foreword

*N*othing stifles the vitality of authentic, spiritual life like cold ritual and cobwebbed liturgy. If our purpose is to live in the vibrancy and spontaneity of the Holy Spirit's fullness, inspiration, and expression in every part of our lives, then we ought to have a healthy fear of mechanical worship and rote prayers.

Yet there are times when the praying saints of God find themselves numbed by crisis—our prayers lack vibrancy and spontaneity. We're hurting, we don't understand our terrible circumstances, we don't know where God is, and we don't know how to begin to talk to him about it. We desperately need help. We need someone to give us voice. We echo what the apostle Paul states in Romans: "... we do not know how to pray..." (Rom. 8:26).

That fact is what moved the divines in the Anglican Church of England to write the *Book of Common Prayer* over four hundred years ago. Those great men of God let others press eavesdropping ears against the doors of their secret places of prayer. They gave to incapable lips the voice of intercession.

I'm grateful for a unique book like *Prayers for Tough Times*. It represents another opportunity to eavesdrop on the inspired heart-cries of men and women of prayer in the practical trenches of life. They have encouraged me, challenged me, motivated me, and drawn me closer to Jesus, the Great Intercessor. I hope that, as you read, they will do all that for you and more.

Ron Mehl

Acknowledgments

My expressions of gratitude must begin with Dan Penwell, my editor and friend, who conceived the idea for this book, chose me to compile it, encouraged as I wrote, and then painstakingly edited the final copy.

I am grateful to Barbara Martin, who wrote twenty-eight prayers and proofed the copy before I sent it off to the publisher, for Petey Prater, who introduced me to her amazing praying friends, wrote twenty-eight prayers, and prayed with me on the phone daily, and for Ron Mehl, my pastor and godly example, who agreed without hesitation to write the foreword, faxing it the day after my initial request.

I appreciate every contributor, the majority of whom are not writers, but pray-ers who simply copied onto paper the prayers they speak daily. They prayed from their own experience—often from their own pain. They prayed for each other as they wrote. They continue to pray for these prayers to bless *you* as you speak them to the Father.

This is the second book Mary McNeil has edited and Andrea Reider has designed and typeset for me. Once again, they both performed superbly. Tricia Toney cleaned and smoothed as she proofread the manuscript. Phillip Rogers' striking cover design completes the package.

Thank you to all.

Introduction

*I*n times of crisis and difficulty, we often feel too wounded and numb to pray. Fear and worry freeze our brains, still our tongues. We hold a cup of coffee and stare into space or curl into a fetal position on the couch. Though we know our only help comes from the Lord, the words don't come; we can't cry out to him.

That's when we call on friends to uplift us, to pray the words that won't form in our brains. Or, if we don't know many praying people, we call the prayer chain at a local church, feeling comforted in the knowledge that they will ask God to fill our needs. We know they will pray the right words, even though we can't.

Wouldn't it be wonderful, though, if we could think how to pray for ourselves during a tragedy or knew how to speak fervent words for friends in trouble? Or form effective words to beg God to lift our nation from disaster and heal it?

This book was written for those terrible times when hope fades and you sink into near-catatonia. It is filled with prayers you can read; prayers to fill your heart with comfort and calm your thoughts; and prayers you can earnestly and fervently pray to the King of kings who has all power, to the God who will hear and help you.

Because of the endless situations requiring prayer, no book could ever cover every circumstance for every person. You may need to scan the table of contents, and then adapt a prayer as you speak it. You may need to change "him" to "her" or "them" to "me." But the content of the prayer, if prayed in earnest, will reach deep into the heart of your Abba Father, who loves you eternally—the God who longs to help you.

In this book, people who spend hours in prayer have joyfully shared some of their prayers with you. They poured their cries to the Lord onto paper for you—so you could pray with them. Prayer comes easily for these men and women because they do it so often. Prayer is their daily habit. The time they spend in prayer polishes their words, tingeing them with eloquence.

Many of the prayers in this book flowed from the band of intercessors who have gathered at Petey Prater's house every Thursday for twenty-five years. Others come from people who partner in twos to pray; still others from people who meet God at home alone in their "prayer closet." These people all have three things in common: they love the Lord, take great pleasure and find contentment from meeting with him often, and desire to pray with you in the pages of this book. They want to help you call out to God in the tough times.

Now, before you begin, would you pray with me?

"Gracious heavenly Father, I know you love me and want to help me through every difficult situation. I desperately need your help, but I know I need to be in right relationship with you before I ask for it. Will you please forgive my sins and be the Lord of my life? We can come to you because of Jesus, amen."

Praying for
Myself

A Wife's Prayer for the First Year of Marriage

*L*ord, help me! I'm married! *Married!* This isn't what I expected at all! I anticipated romantic evenings and thoughtful surprises, but suddenly he's a totally different person than he was before we married. He used to tell me how wonderful he thought I was, now he takes me for granted. I thought we'd be together all the time, instead I rarely see him. Sometimes I wonder if body snatchers sneaked in and replaced the man I love with an alien.

Show me what to do. This is a nightmare. I promised to stay with this man forever! I do love him, but how can I live like this? Is my marriage different than everyone else's? Or is this what everyone meant when they said marriage would be hard work? Teach me how to do this marriage-work, Lord.

I've never felt so lonely in my life. Help me reach out to you for love when I wonder if my husband loves me. Teach me how to show love to him in spite of arguments and disappointments. I know he isn't deliberately hurting me. Release me from my expectations. Help me to be contented with the reality of marriage instead of hoping for a fantasy that exists only in books and movies.

Calm my spirit when we disagree. Show me how to forgive him when he hurts me. Help me understand his point of view. Help us overlook each other's flaws. Teach us how to compromise. Melt us into a unit. I know you can do this, Lord, even though right now the possibility seems pretty remote. I'm asking in Jesus' name, amen.

"Hatred stirs up dissension, but love covers over all wrongs." (Prov. 10:12)

Prayer Concerning the Baby Blues

*D*ear Lord, I feel desperate. I wanted a baby for so long, but now that he's here, part of me wishes I'd never given birth. Part of me understands women who give away their children. I'm so lonely and depressed. I cry all the time. What's wrong with me? Why do I feel so sad?

I know this is supposed to be one of the best times in my life, a time of joy. Sometimes I love holding the baby, stroking his perfect fingers and toes. I love the smell of him and the feel of his head tucked under my chin.

But I'm more exhausted than I've ever been before—right when I need so much energy. I had no idea having a baby would be such work. When the baby cries in the middle of the night, I want to roll over and go back to sleep. I know his baby years will pass quickly; help me enjoy them.

If others are right, and I should see my doctor, then show him how to help me. I depend on you to heal me, Lord. You can wipe away my "baby blues" and teach me how to welcome this new little one. Make me a wise woman who builds her house. Help me remember that my baby is a gift from you; a blessing. Help me to love him with a parent's fervent love—the way you love me. I ask this in the name of your Son Jesus, amen.

"A wise woman builds her house, but with her own hands the foolish one tears hers down." (Prov. 14:1)

A New Parent's Prayer

*L*ord, after months of waiting, he's finally here! What do I do with this little guy? He's so tiny I can hold him in my hands. But he scares me! All of a sudden I'm a parent!

You've given me the privilege of raising this child for you, but I'm not sure I'm up to the task. The baby furniture and fresh coat of paint on the walls of his room seem insufficient preparation for this tiny eternal soul.

Funny. I already love him. I want the best for him. How do I train him to love and obey you? I need the wisdom of centuries! Thank you that I have your wisdom recorded in the Bible.

I feel so unworthy. I want him to follow in your footsteps, but I fear he'll imitate mine. Teach me your love and your ways so I can raise a son who will be your man in his generation. In Jesus' name, amen.

"Train a child in the way he should go, and when he is old he will not turn from it." (Prov. 22:6)

Needing Help with a Difficult Child

*L*ord, your Word says that children are a reward from you, but this child makes me wonder about that scripture. I brought her home from the hospital with such joy and high hopes, never envisioning the challenge she would bring to my life.

She has drained my physical, mental, financial, and spiritual resources. I have worried, prayed, and sought advice from godly professionals. She's exasperated me, embarrassed me, and caused me to question both my parenting *and* my sanity. I love her dearly, but sometimes I don't like her very much. If I've missed a physical or emotional component to this situation, please show me.

Heavenly Father, I ask that *you* love her through me when my love has dwindled; that *your* infinite wisdom guide me, for she has me totally stumped; that *your* strength and patience sustain me, for I have run out of both.

You love her even more than I do, and only you have the power to change her heart. Place within her a hunger and thirst for you and your Word. Help her experience your unconditional love at every level of her being. Replace any rebelliousness with surrender to your lordship. Make a way of escape for her from fleshly temptations. Give her the strength to resist the pull of our worldly culture.

I thank you ahead of time for shaping her into a beautiful trophy to your love, amen.

"Sons are a heritage from the Lord, children a reward from him." (Ps. 127:3)

Prayer from the Bottom of an Empty Nest

*H*eavenly Father, today someone simply mentioned the name of my absent child and I collapsed into heaving sobs, totally out of control in front of a near stranger. I miss my child. I know it's your plan for children to grow up and leave home, so why does it feel like someone ripped off one of my arms? I feel as if I was fired from the most important job I ever held. I loved doing it. This is so hard. Who am I if not a mother? I can't believe more than a third of my life still looms ahead of me. Where do I go from here?

I know she is your child. You just lent her to me for a while. Help me remember that and thank you for your gift. Show me my place in my child's life now. Show me how to love with an open hand—from a distance. Help me not to hold on to a child who needs to leave me behind in order to become mature. Help me cheer her on; help me to be happy for her.

Give me a new direction, Lord, a new purpose, a ministry. Replace my spirit of mourning with an attitude of gratitude and praise. Help me make you the center of my life. In Jesus' name, amen.

"Turn and be gracious to me, for I am lonely and afflicted." (Ps. 25:16)

Prayer for Help During a Move

*L*ord God, I am overwhelmed. I knew moving wouldn't be easy, but it feels like my whole life has been turned upside down. My friends live far away now. Familiar landmarks and streets have been replaced with a landscape I don't recognize. God, will this place ever feel like home to me, or will a part of me always long for the place I just left?

Boxes are everywhere. I don't even know where to start. As I stare at the bare walls, I realize that only you can fill this home with your warmth. Only your presence can make those who enter here feel peace. Bring fulfillment in my life and replace the longings for my old home with enthusiasm for the memories I will make here. May new friendships be born and old friendships continue despite the distance between us. Soothe the ache in my heart as I think about being far away from those I love.

On the days and nights when I feel so lonely, help me to feel your special touch and be reminded that you are always with me. I ask this in the name of your Son Jesus, amen.

"The Lord's curse is on the house of the wicked, but he blesses the home of the righteous." (Prov. 3:33)

Grant Wisdom as I Start a New Business

O God of my life, Solomon asked for wisdom and you gave it to him. The book of James claims if we want wisdom, all we have to do is ask and you'll give it to us, too. Okay, Lord, I'm asking. I need it. Please give me wisdom as I consider starting up this new business venture. I don't want to run ahead of you, Lord, and I can't do it without you. Please show me if you *don't* want me to do this. Warn me of any possible pitfalls I haven't noticed. If you aren't in it with me, it will fail.

If you do approve, though, let me approach it with energy and confidence. You're the Creator of the universe. Grant me wisdom to create this business. You own the cattle on a thousand hills; provide the money I need to give it a solid start. Set the rules for my business and hold me to a standard of rigorous honesty. I determine before you not to compromise when times get tough.

You see into the hearts and minds of people. Point out solid, honest employees to me, and don't ever let me get away with treating them unfairly in order to increase profits. Rather, show me how to reward them for their faithful service. Teach me how to embrace them as family, seeing them with your eyes of compassion, loving them with your love.

Shape this business into a ministry, an outreach that will somehow bless many in your name. I thank you for your generous blessings. In Jesus' name, amen.

"If any of you lacks wisdom, he should ask of God, who gives generously to all without finding fault, and it will be given to him." (James 1:5)

Help Me Cope with a New Pet

Heavenly Father, I asked that you would bring me a new pet when I was ready. And you did! But now I'm not sure that I'll be able to assume the responsibility. It seems so overwhelming after having been without a pet for a while. He demands so much time and effort that sometimes I just want to call his previous owner and ask if she'll take him back.

And yet he is so adorable! I thank you for this precious gift. Help me to be patient with him and to be a kind and encouraging teacher. Help me to never take out my frustrations on him.

Lord, sometimes I find myself wanting him to be like my last pet. His personality is so different, and he's so active. My other pet was such a mellow and comfortable companion. Help me not to compare the two, but to see him as a new and beautiful creation from you. After all, you gave him to me and you know better than I what I need.

Help me adjust to his personality and habits and to want to spend time with him and care for him. Let us be a source of joy for one another and let him feel secure and loved. Guide me, Lord, so that I do him no harm and give him only things that would be good for his health and well being. Thank you for entrusting him to my care, amen.

"And my God will meet all your needs according to his glorious riches in Christ Jesus." (Phil. 4:19)

A Wife's Prayer on Her Husband's Retirement

*G*racious Father, show me how to live through this new stage of life. Part of me loves having my husband home full time, but most of me feels crowded out of my own home. I'm grateful he has time to kick back, but I don't like it when he commandeers areas of responsibility that used to belong to me.

I feel displaced—like I have no home. Television noise jams the house; papers lie strewn across couches and floors. I need alone time; he wants me to go everywhere with him. I feel guilty when streams of resentment rise within me. I have my own life, my own work. Must I give that up? What is my responsibility, Lord? I hate wasting my time in idle pursuits. Yet I don't want to neglect my husband, either, and I know he's lonely. Father, teach me how to enjoy retirement with him. Help me to know when it's all right to "idle away" time with him. I need your help to figure this out.

Give him a purpose, a ministry. Show him ways to use his time productively. Teach him that life is about more than pleasure, more than money. Help him to see that work produces satisfaction, even if you don't get paid for it. Give him a spirit of self-motivation. Let him see things that need to be done, and then give him the desire and energy to do them. Draw him to actively spend his time seeking after you, God, so that the three of us can be an effective team together. I ask this in Jesus' name, amen.

"And we urge you brothers, warn those who are idle, encourage the timid, help the weak, be patient with everyone." (1 Thess. 5:14)

A Prayer for Release from Inferiority

Take all of me, God. Take what hinders me. Perfectionism is my first, middle, and last name. I try to work my way to you—it is exhausting. I can never do enough. I wonder if your grace is sufficient for me and if you love me just as I am, although I know your Word says that you do. Help me. I choose to believe what your Word says about me and not what self or others think. Retrain my mind to believe truth.

I strive to prove that I am worth loving—instead of simply receiving your love as the free gift that it is. You've said that Christ died for me while I was a sinner; so that must mean you accept me even in my sinful state. Help me lay aside guilt, doubt, and fear and accept your love. Help me understand that if I confess my sin and my failures and receive your forgiveness, I will have the approval from you I so desperately want.

I pray, dear Lord, you will bring forth the plan in my life that you have purposed. I'm tired of trying to figure it out. Cause my spirit to choose, believe, and utterly rest upon your Word . . . then I will have confidence and peace. You have said that you are at work in me both to will and to do your good pleasure. I will rest in this truth and in your Son, amen.

"But God demonstrates his own love for us in this: while we were still sinners, Christ died for us." (Rom. 5:8)

Help with Overeating

*G*od, I feel desperate almost every day. I can't control my eating! I am grateful to have food when so many others don't, but eating is my downfall. Living in a country where so many different foods are easily available is both a blessing and a curse.

I feel ugly, unhealthy, and a big, fat failure. You know all the diets I've tried. If I could just avoid food totally, I could be successful! I cook for the family . . . so how can I flee temptation when I'm around food all the time?

I know my body is a temple for your Holy Spirit, and I want to care for it properly. I just don't know what to do anymore.

Give me your power to resist overeating or provide a way of escape from this temptation as you promised in 1 Corinthians.

Your Word tells me that self-control is a fruit of the Spirit. I ask you to build self-control into my character so that I may honor you. I pray in the name of Jesus, who loves me just as I am, amen.

"No temptation has seized you except what is common to man. And God is faithful; he will not let you be tempted beyond what you can bear. But when you are tempted, he will also provide a way out so that you can stand up under it." (1 Cor. 10:13)

Prayer for Release from Guilt

"*H*ave mercy on me, O God, because of your unfailing love. Because of your great compassion, blot out the stain of my sins. Wash me clean from guilt. Purify me from sin.

"For I recognize my shameful deeds—they haunt me day and night. Against you, and you alone, have I sinned; I have done what is evil in your sight.

"Purify me from my sins, and I will be clean; wash me, and I will be whiter than snow. Oh, give me back my joy again; You have broken me—now let me rejoice. Don't keep looking at my sins. Remove the stain of guilt. Create in me a clean heart, O God. Renew a right spirit in me.

"Do not banish me from your presence, and don't take your Holy Spirit from me. Restore to me again the joy of your salvation, and make me willing to obey you.

"Forgive me . . . O God who saves; then I will joyfully sing of your forgiveness. Unseal my lips, O Lord, that I may praise you."

(*from Psalm 51,* NLT)

Help Me Overcome Survivor's Guilt

*W*hy me, Lord? I can't understand it. Why am I alive while others died? Why am I breathing fresh air? Tasting my favorite foods? Smelling pungent odors? Seeing and touching those I love? I know it's not because I'm better than the others.

I feel so guilty. I don't deserve the gift of life you've given me.

I know you're not fickle, and you don't play games with our lives. I know the scriptures that say you love us and that everything that happens is part of your divine plan. You don't always explain why things happen, though, and I can't figure this one out. Help me to trust your Word, which says your ways are not our ways, and your thoughts are beyond our thoughts.

Right now I choose to receive your gift of life with gratitude. Free me from the chains of guilt that bind my heart and mind and spirit. Alert me to the times when Satan would try to re-forge these chains of guilt in my life. You have said if the Son sets me free, I will be free indeed.

Help me to live with joy, with a heightened sense of the preciousness of life, and with the confidence of knowing you have a purpose for me. Transform this episode in my life into a testimony of praise to you. Thank you that the Son has set me free! Amen.

"So if the Son sets you free, you will be free indeed." (John 8:36)

Prayer for Fear of Flying

*D*ear God, I've always been afraid of flying, but with the recent terrorist attacks, my fear has grown. The thought of boarding an airplane terrifies me, even though I know you care enough to be with me and to help me through the flight.

I need your help, dear Lord. Touch my fearful mind and heart. Fill me with your peace. Give me the faith I need to take this trip. Help me sense your hand around me and around the airplane as you hold us up in the sky. Keep my focus on the image of your everlasting arms underneath us. I turn my face toward you, O Lord, as I give you my fear and ask you to replace it with confidence in you and your faithfulness.

I know you want to encourage me to be strong and courageous, just as you have always encouraged your people to trust you during times of fear. I know that nothing can happen to me unless you allow it. I know you will do what is best for me. I choose to believe those truths—to set my mind on them.

Be with me as well as with the pilots, the crew, and the other passengers. Surround us with your love. Fill every heart with your peace. In Jesus' name I pray, amen.

"I sought the Lord, and he answered me; he delivered me from all my fears. Those who look to him are radiant; their faces are never covered with shame." (Ps. 34:4–5)

Prayer Against Fear after Watching a Terrorist Attack on Television

*H*eavenly Father, why am I afraid? Nobody harmed me or anyone I know. I simply viewed the attacks on television, crying and praying for victims and families. I saw airplanes smash through buildings and knew innocent people had been killed in an instant. I watched human beings plunge from flaming buildings to their deaths. I stared in horror as the Twin Towers, symbols of our nation's pride, crumbled in a cloud of dust. I begged for protection for victims fleeing the disaster. They were people just like me, Lord.

Those horrific images that are seared into my memory changed my whole world, God. They destroyed my sense of safety. I feel the vulnerability of our nation; I feel my own vulnerability. Will it happen again, Lord? Next time will it touch my friends and family? Or will you protect us? I know fear comes from Satan, not you, so take the fear from me. I know that you have all power, God, and can do anything you choose.

I trust my family and myself to you. I know nothing can happen to us unless you allow it. I beg for your protection, but at the same time I ask for the grace to submit to your will. And I understand if something terrible does happen, you will lift good from the bad and use it to glorify you. I realize you will be with my family and me, and provide comfort for us through any trouble you allow. In Jesus' name, amen.

"If you make the Most High your dwelling—even the LORD, *who is my refuge—then no harm will befall you, no disaster will come near your tent."* (Ps. 91:9–10)

Help Me Accept the Aging Process

*D*ear Lord, I am terrified of growing old. I've come to understand how much elderly people suffer, and I want to escape that. The gentle term "aches and pains" is just another way of saying "chronic pain bad enough to disturb sleep." I don't want pain, Lord.

I am terrified of dementia—I don't want to become forgetful and confused. I want my mind to remain sharp so I can recognize my children and loved ones. If I am afflicted by dementia, however, and I begin to rant and rave, allow my spirit to remember you.

So often I've heard old people say they don't want to be a burden, but then they are. I don't want my body to grow weak so my children have to care for me. Please, Lord, help me to accept what you give me. I know that you can spare me from this if it is your will. If not, I ask you to strengthen my children for the task ahead.

I know aging and dying are a result of the curse. You would never have chosen that for us. Still, I have to go through it. Help me to finish well. I really want to keep my independence, but if that's not the path I am to follow, keep me from complaining. Make me sweet and gentle. Help me submit to you. Mold my spirit, even as my body breaks down. As my strength fails, give me enough energy to pray. Through Christ, my stronghold, amen.

"Though outwardly we are wasting away, yet inwardly we are being renewed day by day." (2 Cor. 4:16)

Prayer for a Non-Christian to Pray on the Way to Surgery

*G*od, I've never had much time for you, but I'm really scared, and I need your help. Will you help me, God? I know I'm guilty of a lot of things you don't approve of, but I believe your Son Jesus died on the cross for me. I'm asking you to forgive me for my sins and take me to heaven to live with you if something goes wrong and I die in surgery. If I live through this, though, I promise to do my best to obey you and to let you be in charge of my life. I haven't done a very good job handling it by myself, and I know I need your help.

Please help me not to be so afraid, God. When I get depressed and lonely, will you comfort me?

They're coming to take me into the operating room now, so I'm just going to relax and *believe* that I belong to you. I *believe* you will be with me and help me. Thank you, God.

Jesus said, "I assure you, anyone who believes in me already has eternal life." (John 6:47 NLT)

Cry from a Grieving Heart

*M*y God, I call out to you as a child lost and separated from its parent. I know your hand is reaching out to me, yet I feel too grieved to grasp it. My heart feels like an ice pack within my chest. At the same time, my spirit weeps, yes, longs for communion with you, Father God!

Hear me, O God, as I ask you to re-warm my frigid heart. I long to care again. I long to love again. I long to commingle my tears with one who is hurting. Lord, without your help, it would be so easy for me to retreat into myself and care only for providing for my own needs and comforts. Deliver me, O God, from being inconsiderate and indifferent.

I know you have heard my cry, Father, and I thank you now for a heart-wash. I open myself to your love, and I fully expect it to flood me and fill me. Make me long once again to be used in your service. Because of Christ I can pray, amen.

"Weeping may remain for a night, but rejoicing comes in the morning." (Ps. 30:5)

Prayer for the Times I Fail

ear God, I thank you for the words of encouragement you spoke to Joshua long ago when he looked ahead to the seemingly impossible job of leading your people into the Promised Land. You said if he would be courageous and obey you, he would succeed. That promise strengthens me during my own unique times of discouragement.

Nothing seems to work out as I had planned. Unforeseen circumstances block my path. Disappointments abound—both from others as well as myself. What is the use of going on when my plans fall apart and my expectations are dashed to pieces?

Yet I know I can't quit when life becomes too challenging and demanding. I know you want me to be strong and courageous. You want to encourage me. Fill my mind and heart with hope so I can accomplish all of your good purposes for my life. Keep close to me, Lord. Thank you for the assurance of Jesus' words when he said, "Surely I am with you always, to the very end of the age."

Place your hand over my heavy heart. Fill me with the faith I need to take the next step on my pathway. I want to follow you instead of giving up. Please renew me and be with me this day, for Jesus' sake, amen.

"Have I not commanded you? Be strong and courageous. Do not be terrified; do not be discouraged, for the LORD your God will be with you wherever you go." (Josh. 1:9)

A Prayer in Times of Loneliness

*H*eavenly Father, I ache with loneliness. The silence of this empty house screams in my ears. The phone doesn't ring. My mailbox is empty. I feel detached and abandoned by those closest to me. Does anyone care?

Father, when these hollow pangs of loneliness strike, remind me that I'm not ever truly alone. You have promised to be my constant companion—always accessible with never a goodbye. Thank you for the example of your Son, who often withdrew to lonely places to spend time with you.

Restrain me from filling the voids in my life with anything but you. May your everlasting presence occupy the empty places in my heart. Transform my seasons of loneliness into treasured times of fellowship with you.

Lord, thank you for being my forever friend, amen.

"*Turn to me and be gracious to me, for I am lonely and afflicted.*" (Ps. 25:16)

"*Yet I am not alone, for my Father is with me.*" (John 16:32)

Help Me Be Sure
I'll Go to Heaven

O Lord God, what will happen to me when I die? I believe in heaven and hell, and I know I don't want to go to hell. I try really hard to do good things, but I'm afraid I haven't done enough to get me into heaven. I've heard I can't get there by being good anyway, and just thinking about that terrifies me.

People tell me you don't want anyone to go to hell; you want everyone to spend eternity with you in heaven. They tell me the Bible says you sent your Son to die for me so my sins can be forgiven and I can go to heaven. It's hard to believe you would do that for me, Lord.

Still, I *choose* to believe. I *choose* to believe your Son died for me. I ask you to forgive my sins and change me. Make me like you. I *choose* to believe that I belong to you, and I *choose* to believe that you want everyone who belongs to you to live in your home in heaven after they die. Thank you, Lord, amen.

"For God so loved the world that he gave his one and only Son, that whoever believes in him shall not perish but have eternal life." (John 3:16)

Please Don't Abandon
Me in Old Age

"O God, you have taught me from my earliest childhood, and I have constantly told others about the wonderful things you do. Now that I am old and gray, do not abandon me, O God.

"Let me proclaim your power to this new generation, your mighty miracles to all who come after me.

"Your righteousness, O God, reaches to the highest heavens. You have done such wonderful things. Who can compare with you, O God?

"You have allowed me to suffer much hardship, but you will restore me to life again and lift me up from the depths of the earth. You will restore me to even greater honor and comfort me once again.

"Then I will praise you with music on the harp, because you are faithful to your promises, O God."

(from Psalm 71:17–21 NLT)

Help Me Trust You to Provide a Marriage Partner

*L*ord, I've never doubted you would send along the right marriage partner for me. You promised to provide all my needs, but it's been a long time, Lord.

I think of myself as a pretty content person. I work on my relationships with friends and family, and with you. I study to increase my skills, so I'll be the best I can be when my marriage partner shows up. Sometimes, though, I get pretty lonely.

I feel especially bad when people start clicking off my good points as though they're trying to figure out what's wrong with me—why I'm not in a relationship. I could have had romantic relationships, Lord, but I'm waiting for you to send me someone who is sold out to you. (Please forgive me for being superficial, but I'd like them at least marginally good looking. That's not being too picky, is it?)

I know you are powerful, Lord. If you can calm raging waves, I know you can give me a lifelong companion. Firm up my wavering faith; give me patience—or the willingness to remain single if that's what you have for me. If Jeremiah and Jesus could stay single, I guess I can too, but it doesn't feel like I have the gift of singleness Paul talked about. If you're willing, could you send the right person along for me? I'm asking in Jesus' name, amen.

"My soul is in anguish. How long, O LORD, *how long?"* (Ps. 6:3)

Help Me Find a Job

racious God, my provider, I thank you that I need not fear in this difficult time of searching for work. Even in times of economic depression, you sit above the circle of the earth and see every job available. Lead me to that perfect job for me. Give me work that will satisfy my financial needs and allow me to shine forth for you. I'd even be happy with manual labor that would give me time to meditate on you and pray as I work. Open doors, and then give me wisdom as to which door to enter, which advice to take. Grant me favor with the people in charge of hiring.

Keep my mind open as I pound the pavement. Help me to recognize possibilities when I "accidentally" bump into someone with information about a job I never considered before. Make me willing to take jobs I considered menial at one time, if that is what you have for me. Teach me to do it cheerfully and gratefully.

Take away any tendency toward shyness and help me search aggressively, free of fear. Don't let the pain of rejection slow my job search. Continue to remind me that you will provide for me even if you choose not to send along a job right now. You own the cattle on a thousand hills; you have the resources to supply all my needs, and you have promised you will do just that. Thank you, Lord, that I can trust you to keep your word. I have no doubt you will care for me. I praise your name, Lord, amen.

"So do not worry, saying, 'What shall we eat?' or 'What shall we drink?' or 'What shall we wear?' For the pagans run after all these things, and your heavenly Father knows that you need them." (Matt. 6:31–32)

Help Me through This Financial Crisis

The bills are mounting, Lord, and we have so many needs. You've given us much. We live in a land of freedom. We have running water, food, and a roof over our heads, but for how long? I try not to worry, but in trying not to, I think about it even more. Where will we go? What will we do? If we have to move to find work, what about the family and friends who may be left behind? Change seems more frightening than exciting at this point.

Forgive me for worrying. I know it's wrong, and I want to do what's right. I want to be content in all circumstances, but I'm not there yet. I thank you that you look on the heart and know my innermost desire to trust you.

Please build my faith and develop my character so that I can bring help and comfort to my family through this difficult time. Help me to find you in unexpected places and in unexpected ways. Let me always be grateful for your provision, and help me to never take kindness for granted.

You are faithful, Lord, and have promised never to leave or forsake us. Let us know your presence more clearly than ever before. I ask this in Jesus' name, amen.

"If we are faithless, he will remain faithful, for he cannot disown himself." (2 Tim. 2:13)

A Single Mom Prays for Financial Help

*P*recious Lord, I'm on my knees, asking for your help. There are more bills coming in than money. I feel like I'm sinking in a pit and I can't get out. I'm caught in an endless cycle, living from paycheck to paycheck. My head is going under, Lord. I'm drowning in my debt.

Rescue me! Hear my cries! You are my source, Lord, not my paycheck. You are my provider. You own the whole earth, and every good thing I have has come from your hand.

I lay it all down, Lord. I give it all to you: my rent, utilities, car payment, insurance, food, clothing, daycare, everything. Teach me how to handle my finances wisely so that I can bring glory to you and set a godly example for my children. Forgive me, Lord, for the times I've been wasteful and ungrateful with the money you have given me. Speak to the father of my children about the support that he should be providing. Convict his heart without my having to wrestle him into court.

Thank you, Lord, that you will meet all of my needs. I know that you have heard my prayer, and before I've even finished speaking your hand is already at work. I will rest in that knowledge. I pray through Christ who has provided for me, amen.

"And my God will meet all your needs according to his glorious riches in Christ Jesus." (Phil. 4:19)

Prayer for Comfort after a House Fire

*D*ear heavenly Father, we've lost everything. We're grateful no one in our family was hurt, but we've lost all the earthly possessions we held so dear. Years of photographs, newspaper clippings, treasured mementos . . . they were all destroyed by fire. I never knew it would hurt so much to lose these things. I feel as if I've been stripped of my memories.

Take away the depression, Father. Help us to see the new thing you are doing in our lives. You will not leave us homeless and forsaken. Help each member of our family to take one day at a time, to be grateful for what we do have, to be uncomplaining, understanding, and kind to one another. Teach us to look to you for our true treasure. Help us to place more value on what lasts through eternity than on what can disappear in a single disaster.

You are our strength. You are our song. You are our provider and helper. Give us wisdom in this hour, and help us to hear your voice above all others. And in hearing your voice, give us the power and ability to walk in obedience down the road you open before us. Help us not to be sidetracked to the right or the left, but keep us focused on you and faithful to you. In Jesus' name we pray, amen.

"Let us hold unswervingly to the hope we profess, for he who promised is faithful. And let us consider how we may spur one another on toward love and good deeds." (Heb. 10:23–24)

Prayer in the Midst of an Endangered Pregnancy

O merciful Father, have pity on me. I don't understand why you have allowed the life of my baby to be threatened. You know how deeply I love this child, even though I can't see her. She is alive, a tiny person—I feel her moving inside me. I am so afraid for her. Save her precious life, Lord. How can I endure this? Teach me how to trust you. Help me submit to your will.

I want to protect her, but I can't. Her life is your hands. All I can do is lie here in bed, trying not to move, trying to relax. The doctors tell me they are helpless to save her. All we can do is wait, and you know, Lord, I've never been very good at waiting. Give me patience. Help me to focus my thoughts on you, knowing you love her even more than I do.

I determine to have faith in you. I choose to believe you can spare her and bring her into this world as a beautiful, healthy baby. I believe you have great plans for her life. I believe she will grow into a godly woman who will love you fervently and will serve you diligently. I believe her life will bless many people.

Still, if you love her so much you want her to live in heaven with you now, Lord, I trust you about that. I give her to you. I want whatever is best for her, and I know that's what you will do. Help me to confidently rest in that. Thank you for your love, Lord, amen.

"And we know that in all things God works for the good of those who love him, who have been called according to his purpose." (Rom. 8:28)

Prayer Concerning Guilt over a Loved One's Death

I need your help, Lord. I miss my loved one. I don't know why you took her home before I had a chance to explain. The scene of our last time together keeps running through my mind—sad words that can never be erased. Why did you let her die before I could ask for forgiveness? Before I could explain? Why Lord?

Ah, but you've heard that question from me so many times. And how well I know your answer: "Trust."

Lord, I want to trust you. Please help my unbelief. Help me to accept your forgiveness and to understand that my loved one holds no accusation or pain because of unfinished words here on earth. She's with you where all things are good. She holds no bad memories. She's rejoicing and will rejoice even more when I join her. But until that day, wash me free of guilt and help me to approve the good by remembering the lovely times we shared together. Give me the ability to forget the bad times. Help me to recall scenes of laughter and shared dreams.

Thank you that you understand me better than I do myself. It's through you that I am fearfully and wonderfully made. I praise you that you are greater than the rolling emotions I feel in my heart. Give me victory over this, Lord, and let me trust in you, amen.

"For God is greater than our hearts, and he knows everything." (1 John 3:20)

Prayer of a Rape Victim

*D*ear heavenly Father, I'm afraid. I know I don't have to be, but every time I close my eyes, I see the naked ugliness of the man who raped me. The terror is as real as that first moment when I heard his labored breathing and saw evil desire in his eyes. I'm afraid to leave my home. I feel uncomfortable talking with men I don't know. I especially don't want to look into their eyes. I feel dirty and exposed.

I know you want me to rise above this fear, but the man may find me yet. Every small noise sends me looking under the bed, behind the shower curtain, peeking through a window.

Take away my fear, Father, and make me bold. Replace the ugly image of evil with one of your shining glory. Fill me so full of your love that it overflows to everyone I come in contact with regardless of their gender. Tear down my walls of self-preservation. Let me feel the safety of being held in the shadow of your wings. Give me the ability to receive love once again.

For you are great and mighty, Lord. You are able to take this thing that was bad in my life and use it for goodness and honor. Open my eyes to see the new thing you are doing. Let me see the future and hope you've prepared for me. In Jesus' name, amen.

"Forget the former things; do not dwell on the past. See, I am doing a new thing! Now it springs up; do you not perceive it? I am making a way in the desert and streams in the wasteland." (Isa. 43:18–19)

A Prayer from One Falsely Accused

*M*y Lord and my God, I turn to you in my despair. You alone know my heart, and I welcome your examination of my motives. My accusers stand on every side of me wagging their fingers, clicking their tongues, saying untrue things about me.

Lord, I ask you to be my attorney-in-fact. I stand dumbfounded before those who seek to destroy me by smearing my name publicly. They make completely false allegations. Lord, could their perceptions be that skewed?

I have examined my ways, and I stand clean before you. Go before me, Lord. Be my rear guard, flank my sides, and we shall prevail. I seek no revenge, merely justice and a cleared name. I thank you now for defending me and letting righteousness reign. I pray to the One who understands, amen.

"O Lord, you have searched me and you know me. You know when I sit and when I rise; you perceive my thoughts from afar. You discern my going out and my lying down; you are familiar with all my ways. Before a word is on my tongue you know it completely, O LORD. You hem me in—behind and before; you have laid your hand upon me." (Ps. 139:1-5)

O God, My Children Have Been Wrongly Taken by the Authorities

*H*eavenly Father, I cry to you for help and justice. I'm living a nightmare. The children you gave me to nurture and raise have been taken from me by the authorities. I didn't do anything wrong! How could this happen?

Lord, I know that the confusion, lies, and misunderstandings swirling around me are not from you, but from Satan. Render him powerless against our family.

Comfort our frightened children. Protect them from ungodly influences in the homes where they're staying. Let the scripture they've learned strengthen them. Show us how to be godly examples to them in this stressful time. I have so many fears: Will this scar our children for life? What will it do to our marriage? How will we pay the mounting legal and counseling bills? What if I collapse under the stress? At this moment I release to you all these fears. I trust you to work everything out. I also entrust to you our reputation with family, friends, and the community.

Take away my outrage toward those who have perpetrated this injustice, for I know my anger doesn't bring about a righteous life. Give me insight into the people making the decisions in our case. Help me understand the system so I can work within it to regain our children. Lord, you know everything and you are love. As an act of faith, I place my family in your hands, trusting you to work your perfect plan in our lives.

"The angel of the LORD encamps around those who fear him, and he delivers them." (Ps. 34:7)

Deliver Me from Feeling Useless

*L*ord, I fight these feelings of uselessness so often. Sometimes they fill me as a fresh grief, sometimes as a familiar, unwanted ache.

I want to be busy doing things, learning things, contributing to others' lives, expanding my horizons—all those activities that give satisfaction and a sense of personal value. But I can't. I feel so useless!

Please help me to live by faith—faith in your goodness and love and in your plan for my life. Remind me that I *can* fulfill the purpose for which you created me—to glorify you and enjoy you. Help me remember that Jesus commended Mary, who cultivated her relationship with him by sitting at his feet, rather than Martha, her busy sister.

Lord, give me the courage to hope and not give up. Give me the love to value others and not become self-centered or bitter, and the strength to praise you and not complain. And if you would, allow me to enrich and bless the lives of those around me.

I love you, amen.

"'Martha, Martha,' the Lord answered, 'you are worried and upset about many things, but only one thing is needed. Mary has chosen what is better, and it will not be taken away from her.'" (Luke 10:41–42)

Make Me Victorious Despite Chronic Illness

*G*od, the psalms tell us we are fearfully and wonderfully made . . . but my body isn't behaving according to your design. I live day in and day out with the discouragement and frustration of an ailing physical shell. Please heal me if it is your will.

Father, I know there can be various sources of illness. If this sickness is a result of sin in my life, please reveal it to me. I am willing to turn from that sin and obey you. If I'm suffering because of an attack of Satan, I claim the armor of God you have recorded in Ephesians 6. If I am ill so that your reputation may be enhanced in some way, I pray you will glorify yourself through my life.

Perhaps the hardest thing to learn, Lord, is to welcome trials as friends, knowing trials build character, knowing the suffering I endure molds me into the image of Jesus Christ. Help me to be "more than a conqueror" through you. Live your life victoriously through me. I can hardly wait for the day you will give me a new, perfect body to live in for eternity. That perspective makes my time on earth seem shorter and that hope brings me joy today. I pray through the One who has endured trials for me, amen.

"Consider it pure joy, my brothers, whenever you face trials of many kinds, because you know that the testing of your faith develops perseverance. Perseverance must finish its work so that you may be mature and complete, not lacking anything." (James 1:2–4)

Help Me Organize
My Busy-ness

Gracious Father, when I ask you to reveal what keeps me from growing in you, you point to my busyness. I know I take on too much, but whenever someone calls me to volunteer I feel responsible to help. Isn't a Christian supposed to meet needs?

I know you planned my life before I was born; you wrote out all my good works. Show me how to recognize the tasks you created for me. Teach me when a need is not *my* call. Help me to make you Lord of my days so that, with your guidance, I can do the things you've designed for me, rather than rushing through activities someone else chose. O Lord, you didn't expect Elijah to fill every need in Israel when famine swept the land; you know I have to choose from among the many demands and opportunities before me.

Make me determine to set aside a special time each day to read your Word, to talk to you, and then listen. Teach me to respond to the prompting of your Holy Spirit so that I don't step off the path, but instead go where you lead and do your bidding.

Keep me from jamming my life so full I push you out. Help me to make time to sit at your feet and learn from you. Tell me when to say no. Then when the answer is yes, fill me with your power. I ask these things in Jesus' name, amen.

"Jesus said, 'I assure you that there were many widows in Israel in Elijah's time . . . Yet Elijah was not sent to any of them, but to a widow in Zarephath in the region of Sidon.'" (Luke 4:25–26)

Prayer When I'm Faced with Circumstances Beyond My Control

*L*ord, I'm not used to this. I don't know where to go or what to do. I want to fix this, and I can't.

Thank you for the assurance that this situation doesn't knock you off your throne. Your power is not diminished by my helplessness. Your glory is not lessened by my human weakness. I can trust you to act, even though I don't know what to ask you to do.

Somehow my heart is quieted when I concentrate on who you are: Almighty, Compassionate, Sovereign, Beautiful, Deliverer, Excellent, Unchanging, Forgiving, Good, Holy, Living, Just, King eternal, Merciful, Righteous, True, Wise, Friend.

Thank you for the grace to believe. Thank you for the comfort that is mine when I leave this in your hands. In Jesus' name, amen.

"May the God of hope fill you with all joy and peace as you trust in him, so that you may overflow with hope by the power of the Holy Spirit." (Rom. 15:13)

Prayer When I'm Exhausted

*L*ord, I am so tired. I feel that I have given all I have to give, and I am completely empty. Please restore my energy, my hope, and my enthusiasm. Take my discouragement and fling it far from me. Help me to remember that I work for *you* and that you will reward me if I persevere.

Thank you that you do not tire as I do, and your reservoir of love is never depleted. Please let your compassion, kindness, and joy flow into me. Refresh me as I spend these quiet moments in prayer with you. Help me to borrow from your strength now—I feel sapped of the ability to do anything for anyone. Fill up my heart with goodness so that it can once again overflow to others. I thank you for carrying me through this time of weariness. I ask this in the name of your Son Jesus, amen.

"I said to myself, 'I'm completely worn out; my time has been wasted. But I did it for the LORD God, and he will reward me.'" (Is. 49:4 CEV)

Prayer for a Troubled Marriage

*L*ord, everything I do to make my marriage work, fails. My prayers come up empty. When I ask you to change my mate, your small voice whispers that it's me you want to change.

Lord, I didn't come into this marriage to change. I thought I was already doing pretty well. I was mature, open, transparent, communicative, and loving. Wasn't I? But now I find that I'm not quite so mature. Not so open. When my feelings have been hurt, bruised, or even crushed, I withdraw or lash out. I either rationalize my behavior or deny it.

I find that I'm not so loving. How could I be if I hate the one I promised to cherish until I die? All my efforts seem to turn into either bitter arguments or frigid silence. Lord, help me. I don't know what to do.

One thing I've discovered is that I don't know how to love unconditionally. Help me see my mate the way you do, with compassion and forgiveness. Help me be objective. Give me clues to begin to understand my spouse. Help me be loving, kind, gentle, patient, and long-suffering, rather than vengeful. Make me warm, not cold. Give me a soft answer, not a sarcastic one. Teach me to forgive so that I will be forgiven. Teach me to express my feelings in a loving way rather than to harbor bitterness. Make me the partner you want me to be, and make our marriage a reflection of Christ and the church.

"Be kind and compassionate to one another, forgiving each other, just as in Christ God forgave you." (Eph. 4:32)

God, Lift My Depression

*H*elp me, God. I cry to you from this dark place. Everything in my life is blackness, heaviness, sadness. My joy in life is gone; my hope for the future is gone. I lay immobilized day after day, unable to move, to work, to function; unable to care for my family or myself.

Where are you, Lord? Why don't you come and rescue me? I cannot help myself. I cannot even pray or hear your voice. Lift me out of this deep pit. I have tried to find my way out. I've tried to cry my way out, to scream my way out. I am exhausted. Unless you help me, I am finished.

If this testing place is from you, Lord, teach me what it is you would have me learn. Cover me with your mercy and your grace. Help me, Father. Provide the right doctor if that is the solution to this suffocating sorrow.

Send your answer, Lord. Take me by my right hand and pull me to freedom. Restore my life. I'm trusting you to meet my need, amen.

"For I am the Lord, *your God, who takes hold of your right hand and says to you, 'Do not fear; I will help you.'"* (Isa. 41:13)

An Addict's Cry for Help

*O*h God, I am so desperate! I have sunk to the depths. This miserable existence . . . my body and mind decaying, my family alienated, my inability to work . . . I am known by my offenses. My nerves are on edge. I can't rest. Every day I must feed my habit. I scheme, lie, and steal for the next fix. If I don't, I get sick . . . so very sick. I am filled with shame; clothed with guilt.

And yet, you give me breath. And a glimmer of hope to think I can stand firm against the demons that taunt me, that laugh at my efforts to climb out of the pit. I surrender to you, Lord, helpless unless you help me. I need you, only you. I repent for choosing to walk away from all things good and pure, everything honest and true. I abandoned my responsibilities. I walked out of light into darkness. And the darkness is thick, oppressive.

Lord, please forgive my arrogance and pride. Forgive my greed, my love of pleasure that brought only emptiness. Forgive my self-ishness, the irresponsible behavior that robbed those I love of provisions and emotional peace. Forgive me for making others needy so that my needs might be met.

Father, I give you my failures, anxieties, and fears. Thank you that your Son died so I could walk in newness of life. I yield to you now. Come into my heart. Transform me, renew me, fill me with your love and your purpose for my life. Deliver me from this addiction. Nothing is too difficult for you. I praise your name, Lord, amen.

"Therefore, if anyone is in Christ, he is a new creation, the old has gone, the new has come!" (2 Cor. 5:17–18)

A Prayer for Help after Receiving an Eviction Notice

*L*ord, help! We've just received an eviction notice. I don't know how we ended up here, but here we are with no place to go. The thought of my family being out on the street is more than I can bear. I'm so stressed I can hardly function. Where are we going to go?

What will people think? I know I shouldn't worry about that, but I do. I need your peace. I need to remember that you knew this was going to happen and that you're in control. Help me not to look at my circumstances but to trust in you and your Word.

Lord, you are our provider. Please find us a new place to live and the money and jobs necessary to sustain a home. Teach me to seek your kingdom first. I pray that as we go through this storm, you would draw us closer together as a family and closer to you, our source of life. In Christ's name, amen.

"Therefore I tell you, whatever you ask for in prayer, believe that you have received it, and it will be yours." (Mark 11:24)

Prayer While I'm Homeless

*G*od, it's all gone! We have no home. All we have left is this car. How could this happen to my family and me?

How will we survive? How will I bathe the children or brush their teeth? How will we sleep in such cramped quarters? How will we stay warm through the cold nights? Please calm the panic that's numbing my brain and paralyzing my thoughts.

I call upon you as our provider. We are your children and we are in need. Help us, Lord. Lead me to people who will open their hearts to help us. Help me find a place for us to stay, and give me work.

Show yourself strong; overcome this disaster in our lives and bring glory to your name. We trust in you and your goodness right now, even before you've come to our rescue. We praise you for your love and faithfulness and eagerly wait for your answer to this prayer. In Jesus' name, amen.

"The poor will eat and be satisfied; they who seek the Lord *will praise him— may your hearts live forever!"* (Ps. 22:26)

"Jesus replied, 'Foxes have holes and birds of the air have nests, but the Son of Man has no place to lay his head.'" (Matt. 8:20)

Keep Me from Fear of Death

bba Father, I need my Daddy, my God. I am so afraid of dying. It tortures me all the time. Sometimes I dream about it and wake up with my heart hammering. When I hear about some violent attack on television, I imagine it happening to me—and fear rushes at me.

I know I don't need to be afraid. You have forgiven my sins and live in my heart; I know I'll go to heaven if I die. I think I'm terrified of the pain that may come just prior to death. I wonder what is it like? How will it feel? I've never had a high pain threshold. I don't know how to die.

Help me to remember that when death comes, you will walk through it with me, helping me and comforting me. I know you have defeated death, so it can't keep me. You will snatch me from it and transport me to the beauty of heaven where your arms will embrace me. In Jesus' name, amen.

"The LORD is with me; I will not be afraid." (Ps. 118:6)

A Prayer Concerning Midlife Crisis

Omniscient Father, my youth is gone. My middle years loom ahead of me—empty of children, void of accomplishment. I expected to be gliding smoothly along the path of life by now; to my amazement, I find it more complex and difficult than ever. I glimpse my own mortality. But worst of all, I understand I am ordinary. Just ordinary.

I wanted more, God. Is that wrong? Did I crave too much? Where do I go from here? Will a change of career fulfill me? Should I seek out new adventure; more pleasure? How can I make the last half of my life count?

I determine to find my answers in you, Lord. Give me contentment and fulfillment in serving you. Help me remain constant, continuing to make right choices, never failing to keep your commandments. I will not discard my marriage partner, God. It saddens me when I see so many others who do so at this stage of life—it never makes them happy. I will not focus on myself and my problems, instead I will lift praises and gratitude to you without complaint. Show me new ways to serve you. You promised to make me fruitful in old age and, though I don't look forward to growing older, I eagerly look forward to the fulfillment of that promise. I know I will find my significance in you. Because of this, I thank you in the name of your Son Jesus, amen.

"Now all has been heard; here is the conclusion of the matter: Fear God and keep his commandments, for this is the whole duty of man." (Eccles. 12:13)

A Prayer for Strength in Old Age

Gracious heavenly Father,
Give strength for this season of my life.
Lord, give zest, energy enough to hoot and holler,
to relinquish and laugh,
to run in the spirit even if I do not run in the flesh.
Give continued willingness to sweat for you.
Perfect new passions in me; enlarge my vision;
then press me to labor's door
until it moves, until the door swings wide and
it is finished, again, for you.
Do not let me flag;
do not let me fail simply because my hair is gray
and my muscles have grown flabby.
Help me plow and sow and harvest until sunrise
when you pluck me away upward. Amen.

"No one whose hope is in you will ever be put to shame." (Ps. 25:3)

Prayer after a Miscarriage

ear me, Father, please hear me! I feel so lonely, God. Yesterday I had a life moving and growing inside me. Today I am empty. I don't understand. Am I being punished? Would I not be such a good mother to this baby? Are you protecting me from great heartache with this child?

My friends assure me that you provide for these babies. I know in my heart that is true, Lord, but right now I ache. I miss that which I thought was to be. I don't understand any of this. The pain is so deep. The pillow is soggy with tears. How will I get through another day? Will I ever smile again, let alone laugh?

You alone are my solace. Where do I run at times like this? I run to you, Lord, for you collect my tears in a bottle. You hear my cry in the night. Yes, Lord, I trust you with my sorrow. Amen.

"Those who sow in tears will reap with songs of joy. He who goes out weeping, carrying seed to sow, will return with songs of joy, carrying sheaves with him." (Ps. 126:5–6)

Prayer When a Baby Is Stillborn

Oh Lord, our hearts are heavy, burdened with a sadness that envelops us like a smothering blanket. Take it off! Let us wake from the dream that cannot be real; the dream that we want to deny with our whole being. How can our baby be dead? Wasn't it just a few days ago that we felt his body moving within the womb? Was there something we should have known . . . could have done?

Yet, as our tears fall, we fall to our knees and cry, "Abba Father, have mercy!" "Taste and know that I am good," you said. At first the only taste was one of salty tears, then the covering of sorrow lifted and the light of your glory and grace penetrated the density of our grieving. We have Hope! You're our Hope!

We will miss the flesh of our flesh, but we know we will have eternity to get acquainted. What you will is never wrong, even though our finite hearts and minds cannot comprehend it. Trust and obey are the commands that contain the promise of comfort to those who comply. So we choose trust and obedience, as we humbly come to Jesus to be comforted with the supernatural. You only are our expectation; we will not be moved. Even if our faith is shaken, we shall remain upright as you continue to make us holy. We want to be all that you desire; help us not to waste this grief.

As we have said hello and good-bye to our sweet baby, we say, "Nevertheless, your perfect will be done, O my Lord." Amen.

"Hear my cry, O God; listen to my prayer." (Ps. 61:1)

Prayer Following the Death of a Child

*H*ow can I bear this, O Lord? My beloved child, the joy of my life, is gone. I feel as though someone reached into the center of my being and ripped everything out, leaving a hollow, weeping wound. Will the aching emptiness ever heal? Sometimes I wonder if I want it to. I think I'm afraid my beloved child might be erased along with the pain, and I couldn't endure that. If the grief is all that remains of her, I prefer the grief to losing her completely.

Help me accept the reality that she is gone, Lord, even though I don't understand why. Heal me so I can be whole and able to meet the needs of the rest of my family. Help me loosen my grip on the pain and hold onto memories instead. Please keep the image of her face vivid in my memory, God! Don't let it fade from my sight. Imprint the smell of her, the feel of her, and the sound of her laughter on my brain.

And help me reach out for hope. Though I long to be with my daughter, I will wait patiently until you choose to reunite us. Until that time, help me feel your peace. Keep reminding me she's in heaven, waiting for me; we will spend eternity together, never again separated by death. Thank you for the glorious hope we have in you, through Christ, amen.

"I am torn between the two: I desire to depart and be with Christ, which is better by far; but it is more necessary for you that I remain in the body." (Phil. 1:23–24).

Prayer When a Teen Dies

God, everything in me screams, "Not a teenager!" Death is for the old, not for vibrant young people who have barely tasted life. I loved this young man. His death leaves a tremendous, aching hole in my heart. Every day I turn around expecting to see him, but he's not there. My heart breaks when I think of all the times we'll never share; all the dreams he'll never fulfill.

Lord, the Bible says you number our days. In my grief, help me come to grips with the false expectation that we will all live to old age. Help me remember this young man's life was not cut off too soon; he was not cheated of a full life. He lived the length of time you determined for him before he was born. He fulfilled your purpose for him here on earth.

On the days when I'm angry at you for taking him, remind me that you know the pain of losing a son to an early death. But your Son did fulfill your glorious purpose for him. In your mercy, show me something of your purpose for this young man's life.

Help me draw comfort from your Word and from the fact that because your Son conquered death, this painful separation is temporary; not permanent. Direct me to look beyond this life and my loss. Thank you for the assurance that his life with you in heaven is so fantastic that he really wouldn't want to be back here on earth. In the name of your risen Son, amen.

"Your eyes saw my unformed body. All the days ordained for me were written in your book before one of them came to be." (Ps. 139:16)

Prayer after a Sibling Dies

*H*oly Father, I know you are real. I believe you exist. Yet I am confused. Why has my sister been snatched away by death? She was so young and innocent—just beginning to bloom and grow into the person she would become. I don't understand. Is my sister in heaven? Why won't you answer me, Lord?

I've never faced the death of someone I love before. I don't know how to react. How I should behave? I feel so guilty. We lived in the same home and yet there was so much about my sister I never took time to know. So many things left unsaid; so many things left undone. I never really even looked her in the eye and said, "I love you." Forgive me for wasting so much of our time together.

And God, if I don't know where she has gone, how can I know what will happen to me when I die? Help me find answers to my questions. Help me comfort the rest of the family. Teach me what to say when I happen upon other family members who are crying or struggling with depression. Help us help one another, God. Move us through this mind-numbing grief to find some semblance of normality again. We don't want to dishonor our loved one by forgetting her, but Lord, help us go on with our lives. Help us have joy again. Help us find answers to our questions about death and heaven and eternity, amen.

"I will turn their mourning into gladness; I will give them comfort and joy instead of sorrow." (Jer. 31:13)

Oh God, My Parent Is Dying

eavenly Father, I need your help. Mother is dying and I must go be with her. Don't let her die before I have time to get to her side. We need one last time to talk, to hold each other, and to say goodbye before she is gone. Lord, I feel so anxious; so inadequate. I'm afraid that I won't be able to cope with this difficult situation. Help me know what to do, Lord. Go with me. Cause me to be all I should be for Mom and the rest of the family.

Sit beside Mom as she lies in the hospital bed, Lord. Be with her when she is in pain and discomfort. Quiet her restlessness. Surround her with compassionate nurses and doctors who will be able to make her comfortable. Don't let her suffer.

Lord, Mother hasn't shared with me whether she is ready to die. I want to talk with her about her soul, but I don't quite know how. Go before me; prepare her heart. Give me Bible verses to share that will help her understand your plan for her life. Show her through your Word that you died for her sins. Help us pray together, asking you to forgive her sin and take her to heaven when she dies. Then we will be together again someday. Help me let her go.

Thank you, Lord. I can do all things as you give me the strength, amen.

"I tell you the truth, whoever hears my word and believes him who sent me has eternal life and will not be condemned; he has crossed over from death to life." (John 5:24)

Prayer for a Dying Husband

Oh God, don't let this one I love with all my heart die! Raise him up to life again, Father. I don't want to lose him. This is too difficult. Everything in me cries, "No!" How can I live and function without my husband?

Right now, touch my husband with your healing hand. Your power has raised men and women from the dead; raise my husband from his sickbed, Father. I believe; help my unbelief. Enter that sick room, Great Physician. Touch and heal and restore health. Nothing is too hard for you, Lord. Ease his pain, strengthen him, and help him begin eating again. Direct the path of each one who takes care of him. Let them be gentle and loving. Help them understand what he needs. Stay with him when I cannot be beside him, Lord.

Oh God, help me, too. Quiet my anxious fears. I am in a daze; unable to cope with the simplest daily tasks. Clear my mind. Help me accomplish everything that must be done.

I know you are a God of Love—a God who only chooses the best for me; for us. Make me willing to have your will in my life. I'm so afraid you'll take him from me, Father, but I lay him on your altar and ask that your will be done. Lead me through this wilderness, Lord. Walk with me through this deep valley, as you walk with others when they are needy. Thank you, Lord. I know you hear and answer prayer. Amen.

"Even though I walk through the valley of the shadow of death, I will fear no evil, for you are with me." (Ps. 23:4)

Prayer When a Wife Dies

ear Father, I come to you this morning with something new to me. My heart is broken with the loss of my precious wife. After so many years of enjoying the privilege of having her right by my side, enjoying every minute, making plans for the future, and experiencing everything a happy couple enjoys, she can never be a part of my life in the same way again.

Thank you for allowing me so many wonderful memories of her: her great love of life, her many talents, her desire to faithfully serve you. Thank you for the love she unselfishly showed to each of our beautiful children.

I'm so grateful from our very early childhood years, we both knew you were always there; we could come to you anytime. We've always known that your mercies never cease, your compassion never fails, and your faithfulness never diminishes. Your mercies are new every morning.

Thank you for being the God of all comfort. The days and nights get long and lonely. Grief wants to come in and take its toll, yet I know you are there. My greatest hope is the blessed assurance that my wife is waiting in heaven for the day you will call me to join her.

Thank you for your love that knows no measure and the blood of Christ that washes away all sin. In Jesus' name, amen.

"Because of the LORD's great love we are not consumed, for his compassions never fail. They are new every morning; great is your faithfulness." (Lam. 3:22–23)

Prayer after the Break-up of a Cohabiting Couple

*M*erciful Father, I feel sick; I feel confused. I can't work. I've shed buckets of unmanly tears. I was certain we would marry, Lord. I thought she was the perfect mate for me. I fully expected to spend the rest of my life with her.

Even though I knew the Bible condemned our actions, I didn't believe what we were doing could possibly be wrong. It felt so right. We even attended church together. Every minute with her excited me, thrilled me, and filled me with contentment. I've never experienced that kind of intimacy with anyone else.

But now I feel wounded and unclean; my emotions are festering sores. Will I ever feel whole again? I long for peace. I long for purity. Help me! Forgive me for ignoring your laws and trying to fill my own need for a woman instead of waiting for you to provide a holy relationship for me. Don't let my weakness lead me into this kind of sin again. Don't let me rush into a wrong relationship because I'm afraid you won't send the right wife for me. I pledge myself to remain chaste until marriage, God. I refuse to sin against you and my own body in that way again.

Please fill the hollow places in my soul with your presence. Teach me that you are enough. You will comfort me and lead me out of this pain and loneliness. With your help I will get past this. You will cleanse me and make me pure again. Thank you, precious Lord, amen.

"So I say, live by the Spirit and you will not gratify the desires of the sinful nature." (Gal. 5:16)

Heal the Rift
in Our Friendship

O Lord God, I can hardly believe that my friend, who I have loved dearly for years, could hurt me so badly. We've worshiped together, laughed together, and prayed for each other. I love her as fervently as I love my own sister. Why would she do this to me? Did I do something to precipitate it? Did I hurt her without knowing it, causing her to seek revenge?

I tried apologizing even though I didn't think I did anything wrong. She didn't want to listen. She refused to discuss it. Reveal the source of the problem to me, Lord. Show me how to make peace with her. Should I follow the instructions of Matthew 18 and take a neutral party with me to talk to her about it? I don't know what else to do.

Lord, if she refuses to reconcile and continues to treat me badly, help me forgive her. Let me see her through your compassionate eyes, as a wounded creature you love and wish to restore. Nudge me to pray for her often. Teach me when to let the matter drop so that you will have time to heal it. Make me willing to turn it over to you and wait patiently for your solution. I believe that you will answer my plea for help. Help me understand what it is you are trying to teach me through this. I pray this in Jesus' name, amen.

"If it is possible, as far as it depends on you, live at peace with everyone."
(Rom. 12:18)

Prayer Following the Death of a Pet

*D*ear heavenly Father, I know there are a lot of people who wouldn't understand the grief I am feeling over the loss of my beloved pet, but you do. You watch over all animals. Matthew says you see every little sparrow—so I know you loved my pet, too.

You created animals for our pleasure . . . and she certainly gave me pleasure. She filled many of my lonely moments. She always accepted me without complaint. She never noticed my flaws. Sometimes she made me laugh. She would press up against me and give me physical affection I don't always get from people.

I know your Word doesn't say if the spirits of animals ascend to heaven or not, so I won't know for a long time if she is waiting for me there. Even if she's not, I want to thank you for letting me enjoy her for this brief time on earth. I believe my grief is a tribute to her importance in my life. Please comfort me and heal my pain. In Jesus' name, amen.

"Look at the birds of the air; they do not sow or reap or store away in barns, and yet your heavenly Father feeds them." (Matt. 6:26)

Take My Broken Dream, Lord

*L*ord, I feel like a child coming to her father with a broken snow globe. My dream is broken, Lord, and I feel so discouraged. So disillusioned. I thought I'd heard from you. I tried to pay close attention to your voice; tried to be obedient. Yet my dream shattered into tiny pieces around my feet. What was I thinking? Was it wrong? Is that why you had to wrestle it from me? Was I holding too tightly? Were my motives impure?

Or Lord, have you wrestled my dream away in order to give me something bigger? You are the Father of dreams. You gave them to Abraham, Israel, Joseph, Nehemiah, Daniel, Peter, and John. You long to spark the desire in us to do something beyond ourselves; something so big that only you could make it happen. And then, Father, when all hope is lost, when our snow-globe dream lies in a million pieces on the floor, you move miraculously to make the dream come true.

Help me to focus not on the dream, but on the giver of dreams. Help me to see your leading in this rejection. Fill my heart with peace. Help me to trust your care for me. And then Lord, let me trust you for a new dream. Keep me listening. Help me to yearn for obedience. Help me to see you fulfill my dreams in your time; in your way. And when the day comes that others notice, help me not to take a single ounce of credit for what you have done in my life. Through Christ who has made dreaming possible, amen.

"Now to him who is able to do immeasurably more than all we ask or imagine, according to his power that is at work within us, to him be glory . . . throughout all generations, for ever and ever." (Eph. 3:20)

Praying for
Others

A Prayer for My Child's First Day of School

*P*recious Lord, thank you that you never sleep. Your watchful eye is always upon us. I'm so grateful for that as I send my little one off for the first day of school. Lord, I remember so well how nervous I felt on my own first day— the butterflies in my stomach, the excitement of getting to wear new school clothes, and the uneasiness at being away from home and mom for the whole day.

I pray for a special blessing on my child today. I pray for peace to replace any anxieties.

I pray for ease in making new friends. I pray for a clear mind to be able to absorb all of the new things learned. I pray for patience and understanding for the teacher, and I ask that they relate well to each other.

Thank you, Lord, that you are our perfect Father and I can rest in the knowledge that even though my child will be out of my sight, he will always be in yours. In Jesus' name, amen.

"But from everlasting to everlasting the LORD's love is with those who fear him, and his righteousness with their children's children." (Ps. 103:17)

Give My Child Favor with Schoolmates

ather, my child is suffering. I am too. Her school-mates taunt her, making fun of her clothes, her looks, and her grades. Their cruelty not only wounds my child, it's driving a knife into my heart. I want to shake them, shout at them, give them a dose of their own medicine, and take their parents and the teacher to task.

You know the pain of witnessing the mockery and rejection of your Son. Yet you've told us to love our enemies; to pray for those who persecute us.

Please forgive my anger at these children. Help me see them from your point of view—as little sinners whom you love. Show me how to assure my child of her value in your eyes and mine. Help me explain how sin in each of our hearts hurts others.

Furnish me the words to pray for my child's enemies. Give me ideas for counteracting their behavior in a positive, loving way—overcoming evil with good. Help me know when to intervene.

Lord, my greatest fear is that these children will destroy my child's belief of her innate value. Please use this situation to strengthen her character instead. May she grow in your favor. In the name of your precious Son who valued her enough to die for her, amen.

"But I tell you: Love your enemies and pray for those who persecute you." (Matt. 5:44)

"Bless those who persecute you; bless and do not curse." (Romans 12:14)

Asking for Help with Schoolwork Struggles

*L*ord, you created this child just as he is, including his brain and his unique way of looking at the world. He tries so hard and it's discouraging for him when he doesn't understand his schoolwork.

Develop in him a positive attitude—tenaciousness and patience—that will help him persevere in his struggles with his assignments. Open up other areas in life where he can experience success.

Help his parents and teachers discover the source of the problem and develop creative solutions. Direct them to resources and people who can help. Give them the wisdom to know when to encourage, when to back off, and when to be firm.

Most of all, help them to love him unconditionally, remembering he is already precious in your sight and his value does not depend on success at school.

In the name of Jesus, who loves all his children, I pray, amen.

"Consider it pure joy, my brothers, whenever you face trials of many kinds, because you know that the testing of your faith develops perseverance. Perseverance must finish its work so that you may be mature and complete, not lacking anything." (James 1:2–4)

Help My Overly Sensitive Child

*L*ord, you see my child crumpled here in my arms, sobbing. She takes others' words and actions to heart and is so easily wounded. You know her spirit and her soft heart toward you. How you must have smiled when you created her! She's like a delicate crystal vase—beautiful and fragile. You know how little it takes to make her eyes shine; how little to crush her heart.

God, it tears me apart to see her hurting. I want to wrap her vulnerable spirit in the thick padding of my love and protection to prevent unnecessary pain from others' cruelty and thoughtlessness; to guard her from those who would prey upon her perceived weakness.

But Lord, I know that is not your way. Put your arms of love around her. Strengthen her spiritually, physically, and emotionally. When she feels weak, remind her to ask for your divine strength so she will become strong.

Give her the confidence of your unconditional love, and the courage to face others without wavering. Develop in her an inner reliance on you so she can withstand life's hard knocks and the wily schemes of the evil one. Most of all, may her life shine with the light of your presence, brilliantly reflecting the many facets of your love. Through Christ, amen.

"But he said to me, 'My grace is sufficient for you, for my power is made perfect in weakness.' Therefore I will boast all the more gladly about my weaknesses, so that Christ's power may rest on me. That is why, for Christ's sake, I delight in weaknesses, in insults, in hardships, in persecutions, in difficulties. For when I am weak, then I am strong." (2 Cor. 12:9–10)

A Prayer for My Child in Crisis

ather, my son is in crisis. He's hurting, Lord, and I ache when he hurts. You know how I lie awake trying not to worry. Trying to pray. Trying to trust you. And in some moments I succeed, Lord. In others, I fail miserably. Help me believe in your goodness when it comes to my kids. I would spare him this crisis if I could, but you have not spared him, and I know you well enough to know that you do nothing without purpose. I ask that you accomplish your mighty purpose in my son's life.

Lord, my son feels like your kids did when they left Egypt—hemmed in on one side by a powerful Egyptian army and on the other by a vast sea. You showed your children the way through the trial; show my child. Lead him through obstacles with the same great faithfulness you showed to your chosen children. Teach him to follow you without question; wherever you lead.

Give him ears to hear your voice—wise counsel in the midst of endless foolishness. Give him stamina, Lord, the strength to keep believing when he doesn't see answers.

Give me wisdom to pray beyond my own reason. Give me the endurance to fight for the godly good of my son; that he survives this trauma as a man fully armed for the work you have for him to do. Keep me from giving up. Keep me praying. I ask in my Savior's name, amen.

"But from everlasting to everlasting the LORD's love is with those who fear him, and his righteousness with their children's children." (Ps. 103:17)

A Prayer for a
Rebellious Child

*M*ighty God, once again we fall to our knees, both in reverence and weariness. Hear our cry, O Lord. The behavior of this self-focused, rebel child baffles me. I try to understand; I think I listen—yet I am accused of not caring and trying to control! Father, I know how I raised this child and this thing puzzles me. His early years were so joy-filled. He seemed to take by faith the truths he heard from me. His father and I guided him the best we could. Then parenting started to get harder as he began to question—everything!

Lord, turn his heart to you. I want to spare him the grief of walking without you. Why won't he embrace you and walk in the peace you provide? The laughter he used to draw from his father and me has changed into copious tear spilling. I know he must find his own way, and I plead for you to draw him back to you. As he searches for fulfillment, Lord, may your sweet Holy Spirit be a constant companion and friend. I look to that day when our family will celebrate and give thanks *together* for your saving power, your hand of blessing, and your patience.

Meanwhile, I lay this defiant child on the altar as a surrendered offering. Our parenting continues, but I give you the authorization do whatever it takes to bring this young one back into line. His father and I wait expectantly as you work it out and we, with you, walk it out in Jesus' name, amen.

"For this son of mine was dead and is alive again; he was lost and is found."
(Luke 15:24)

Guide Our Young Adult
As She Leaves Home

J pray to Jehovah-Jireh, the Lord Who Will Provide, for my newly independent child. She has been ours to love and care for since you placed her in our arms years ago. We have clothed, fed, loved, and counseled her. Now, too soon, she is leaving.

Mighty Helper, go with her; stand beside her at every point of need. Be involved in the selection of her roommates; direct her regarding which job to pursue. Help her sift through the false teaching and liberal thinking. Walk with her, Spirit of Truth. Keep her mind and heart and will centered in your Word.

Guide her as she chooses new friends, Lord, perhaps even a husband. Let them be wise and compassionate—young men and women who make truth and faith their only choice. Keep her physically safe. Help her handle each problem she faces with prayer and self-discipline, whether it is loneliness or a difficult exam.

Free us to let her go. Fill our empty hours with worthwhile activities. Though she is far from us physically and we have less time together, keep us close emotionally. I lay my daughter back in your arms, Lord. Thank you for the privilege of being her parent. I know you will go with her and keep her in all places, amen.

"Train a child in the way he should go, and when he is old he will not turn from it." (Prov. 22:6)

Prayer after a
Child Is Injured

*C*ompassionate Father, I bring to you a family so numb and afraid words won't come when they try to pray. Their precious child was injured in a terrible accident and they don't yet know the outcome. Give them peace and family unity, God. Help them draw closer to each other and to you, knowing that you have all power and can do anything. You work out everything for good. Show them how to rest in you as they wait, trusting you. Let them feel your love wrap around them. Keep fear, blaming, and resentment far away. Don't let bitterness add to their distress. Help them give you all their anger at whoever caused this accident. Grant wisdom to the doctors.

Hold the child in your arms, Father. Let health flow from you into him. Banish any permanent bodily injury or brain damage. Mend broken bones; knit torn tissue; ease his pain; speed his healing. Give him a deep relationship with you, Lord. Draw this child so close he feels fused to you. Surround him with your peace and love. Give him a bright future. I pray through the healing name of Jesus, amen.

But God, if you choose to allow the unthinkable, give the family grace to release their beloved child to you, knowing that you love him . . . and them. You *will* be with them always.

"He welcomed them and spoke to them about the kingdom of God, and healed those who needed healing." (Luke 9:11 NLT)

Help This Blended Family

ather God, I bring a family with stepchildren to you, begging you to help them. In the heat of romance this couple thought blending their families would be easy. They thought they could love each other's children, Lord. Both the husband and the wife anticipated that their spouse's children would at least like them, but it hasn't turned out like that.

Lord, it's tough. The children think the stepparents want to usurp the roles of natural parents. They are openly rebellious. Resentment comes to the forefront. It's causing great agitation in the home, and each stepparent has now come to realize they don't love their stepchildren as much as they love their natural children. The home has become a miserable place, Lord, with bitter fighting.

Lead the parents to have utter dependence on you . . . admitting they've made a mess of things. Open their hearts to know that you can and will help. You are their only hope, God. Banish arguing and resentment from their home. Make them willing to compromise and show consideration to each other. Draw them to look for the best instead of blaming and finding fault. Enable them to begin thinking of themselves as a family, overlooking faults, loving each other with your pure love. Infuse the home with your spirit of peace. We know you can do this, Father, so we ask for it in Jesus' name, amen.

"How good and how pleasant it is when brothers live together in unity!" (Ps. 133:1 NLT)

Prayer of a Foster Parent

*D*ear Lord, thank you for the quiet of morning where I can rest in your presence and renew myself before our home bustles with the business of raising youngsters. I am overcome with gratitude that you chose me to minister love to these hurting ones. At the same time I feel inadequate and overwhelmed. I hate to admit I sometimes struggle to love them as much as I love my own children. Change my heart, Lord. Help me to love them fervently and wholeheartedly.

They've been so damaged, God; so neglected. They don't know who to trust; who they can depend on. Make me a tower of strength for them. Send them to me when they need a hug or a pat on the head, and make me willing to put my own interests aside to give them the time they need. Mold me into an example of your pure and holy love. Teach them to recognize you because they see you shining through me. Call them to confess their sins and accept you into the hearts so you can heal them from the inside out. Teach them to give their hurts and concerns to you. Give them a strong relationship with you that will sustain them when they return to their natural families.

God, you know I can't do this alone. Please guide me as I go through this day. Give me patience and divine intuition to know what each child needs. Let every detail of our interactions glorify you. Make us victorious, through Christ, amen.

"So whether you eat or drink or whatever you do, do it all for the glory of God." (1 Cor. 10:31)

Prayer for a
Special Needs Child

*D*ear Lord, it's exhausting parenting a child with special needs. Today, I feel overwhelmed by everything and cannot stop crying. Finding the right resources to help my child is confusing. There are no clear road signs to show me the way. It is intimidating to ask professionals for help. They use terms that I do not understand. Lord, I am hopelessly inadequate. I beg them to help me and they don't. My emotions shift daily like the wind. One day, I feel misunderstood; the next determined and hopeful. Lord, give me the strength to go on.

Your Word is my compass. I am lost without its direction. It gives me comfort. Through it, you give hope to all generations. You meet us at our point of need, no matter where we are. Neither I nor my child has escaped your notice. We are not a bother to you.

As I imagine my child sitting in your lap covering your face with wet kisses, tears fill my eyes. Lord, forgive me for not trusting you with my children. Help me not to give up because the road is hard. Teach me to reflect compassion and forgiveness toward others, even when I feel broken and discouraged. Light my path each day with wisdom. Supply the extra strength and courage needed to run the race that is set before me.

"Let the little children come to me, and do not hinder them, for the kingdom of heaven belongs to such as these." (Matt. 19:14)

Prayer for a Family with a Disabled Child

*H*eavenly Father, my heart grows heavy whenever I think of this family whose child is disabled. They love this young one, Lord, maybe more than they would a healthy child. It breaks their hearts to see her suffer, to know she will never be able to do and achieve all the things most of us take for granted. They agonize when strangers are rude or ridicule her. I know they ask themselves why—why our child, Lord? They would rather bear the pain of the disability in their own bodies than see her anguished and in agony.

Help them, Lord. Strengthen them when they are so exhausted they don't want to continue doing all the work required for her care. Keep them from guilt because her helplessness sometimes angers them. Lift the financial burden her disability brings, and provide for them.

Draw them close to you and help them pass on your comfort and hope to their daughter. Let your power surge through them, shaping them into uncomplaining servants with hearts that desire nothing less than your will. Enable them to trust you to do whatever is best for them, no matter how bad the circumstances may seem. You will walk with them. I know they are more precious than gold to you. They are your treasure. Thank you for my friends, Lord, and thank you for your amazing love for them, amen.

"But we have this treasure in jars of clay to show that this all-surpassing power is from God and not from us." (2 Cor. 4:7)

Prayer for My Son and the Older Woman Who Seduced Him

O God, how do I pray for this older woman who has seduced my son? I am angry. I am sickened. She is brash and bold like the woman in Proverbs whose house leads young men to the grave. Break her hold on him. Extricate him from this foul smelling sin against his own body. Open his eyes to see the truth of this disgusting relationship.

I know my son is of age, Lord. I don't excuse his actions, but I beg you to strengthen his character. Turn his heart to you. Replace his backbone of straw with a backbone of steel. Replace lustful imaginations with godly thoughts. Make him willing to endure loneliness rather than step into the spiritual and emotional manure of an affair with a woman who has children.

And though I can hardly stand to think about her, merciful Father, I will pray for her because you have instructed us to pray for our enemies. I know you love her and want a relationship with her, so I pray for you to heal her soul, Lord, by calling her to you. Save her so that she will be ashamed of her way of life and begin to obey you. Do this in the name of Jesus.

And in your mercy, God, save my son. Through Christ I beseech you, amen.

"I saw among the simple, I noticed among the young men, a youth who lacked judgment." (Prov. 7:7)

"Many are the victims she has brought down; her slain are a mighty throng." (Prov. 7:26)

Rescue Children from Sexual Abuse

*M*erciful Father, rescue the young girls and boys across this nation who seek love and find abuse instead. Have pity on them, Lord. Grant them justice. Give them the courage to speak up and tell someone the awful things they endure at the hand of an adult who pretends to care about them. Help the children to be believed, not accused or ignored. If they tell another child, press that child to speak to a responsible adult. Give the adult proof of the crime and the courage to save the child. Place the children in a safe, loving environment where they can learn about healthy human love and about your love, Father.

Send people of wisdom to comfort and teach them; normal loving adults to fill their needs. Don't let the actions of one wicked person twist their lives, instead, let your pure love shine brightly in their hearts. Heal them completely. Make them understand and believe they are innocent victims who have no need to feel guilty. Help them banish the pain brought on when memories flood back by turning over all pain and desire for revenge to you. When pictures of past abuses flash into their minds, render them impotent and unable to cause emotional turmoil. Let the children see them as flat black-and-white photos that have no power. Help them forgive and look forward to a bright future as your beloved children. Bless them, Father. In Jesus' name, amen.

"He felt great pity for the crowds that came, because their problems were so great and they didn't know where to go for help." (Matt. 9:36 NLT)

Prayer for Unsaved Parents

O gracious Lord and Savior, my heart bubbles over with gratitude for your mercy and love. Who am I that you would love me? I am astounded that you would adopt me into your family! You are my Abba Father; my Daddy.

But Lord, my heart aches for my earthly father and mother. They don't know you. They don't want to hear about you. They can't understand why I love you. How could they be so blind? My parents are spiritually ignorant and I thought they knew everything! It breaks my heart. I see the turmoil in their lives—the discontent, the resentments they can't conceal. They haven't accepted your peace. They don't want to know you.

But you long for them to know you. Allow me to have a part in leading my parents into the ark of your love. Give me opportunities to share you with them. Let me speak loving, gentle words that they won't view as abrasive and confrontational. Reach in and squeeze their hard hearts, Lord. Warm them and shape them. Give them a fervent desire for you. Let us belong to the same spiritual family as well as the same earthly family. I know you want to do this, so I ask for it in Jesus' name, amen.

"Go into the ark, you and your whole family, because I have found you righteous in this generation." (Gen.7:1)

Prayer for an Unsaved Friend

ear God, I feel so grieved and burdened for my unsaved friend. He can't recognize Truth because Satan has obscured his mind with a veil of lies. My friend doesn't know you and as far as he is concerned, he doesn't need to know you. He scoffs at the idea that he could be headed for hell and gets angry if I even mention your name.

Snatch away the veil, Lord. Soften his heart. Help him recognize your Truth. Send your convicting Holy Spirit to hover over him. Convict him as he goes about his daily activities, convict him as he sleeps at night, and convict him every time he indulges in sin. Show him that sin is simply a cheap imitation of all the good things you have for him. Bring events into his life which require more than his own strength and understanding. Remove all complacency. Force him to recognize his weakness and his desperate need for you. Banish his rebellious spirit. Make him long for you.

Send people who love you wholeheartedly into his life. Then prepare me, along with those other believers, to reflect your love, power, and grace to him. My desire for my friend is a share in your eternal inheritance. Please save him. In Jesus' name, amen.

"This is good, and pleases God our Savior, who wants all men to be saved and to come to a knowledge of the truth." (1 Tim. 2:3–4)

Prayer for an Unbeliever
Who Fears Death

O God, who fervently loves all people, my friend has told me she is terrified of death. Fear of it haunts her through daily activities; nightmares awaken her in the middle of the night. No matter what she does, she can't shake the feeling of horror. She came to me because she knows I am a Christian. She wanted me to comfort her, Lord, but I couldn't.

She should be terrified of death, Lord, because she's living her life without you, and without you she will spend eternity in torment. God, help her! Don't remove her fear; increase it. Inflate the fear in her heart until she feels as though she will explode unless she turns to you.

Then give her hope. Supply me—or someone else—with words that are precisely right for her; words that will open her mind to understand you and your love for her. Or call her to open your Word and read for herself. Show yourself strong to her. Take away any doubt that you exist. Help her believe you chose her and are stretching out tender arms to her. Call her to invite you into her heart as Lord of her life.

The instant she chooses you, Lord, flood her with peace. Remove every trace of fear. Give her a vision of heaven and an eagerness for her eternal home. Thank you for prompting her to share this with me, Father. Remind me to continually lift her up in prayer. In Jesus' name, amen.

"In my Father's house are many rooms . . . I will come back and take you to be with me that you also may be where I am." (John 14:2–3)

Praying about a Friend's Insensitivity

*L*ord, he did it again! I cringe at the way my friend's insensitive words and behavior wreak havoc with others' lives. He batters with his words and wounds with his thoughtlessness.

Open his eyes. Show him the pain he's causing. Pierce his heart with remorse. Place within him a desire to change. Then draw him to yourself. Save him if he does not know you. Assure him of your love. Reveal to him the strongholds of sin in his life that may be the source of his behavior: anger from past hurts in his own life, selfishness, a bad role model, or faulty thinking.

Bring alongside him those who can lovingly guide him to the transforming power of your Holy Spirit and your Word. Form him into your image so that he'll experience the joy of being like you, learn to encourage others, and cause many to marvel at your greatness.

Thank you that your power can accomplish in us what we cannot do ourselves. In your powerful name, amen.

"All kinds of animals, birds, reptiles and creatures of the sea are being tamed and have been tamed by man, but no man can tame the tongue. It is a restless evil, full of deadly poison." (James 3:7–8)

Prayer for the Family of a Suicide Victim

*G*od of all comfort, someone who was loved and cherished has committed suicide. He has left an empty void in his anguished family. Hold them in your arms. Comfort them in this awful time. Steady their weak knees. Quiet their shuddering, trembling hearts. Balm of Gilead, wipe this terrible scene from their minds and spirits. Send friends and neighbors with warm food, shoulders to cry on, and arms to encircle. Send people who know how to serve silently, when silence is appropriate.

Lord, you are the Master Counselor. Guide them through the maze of legal work. Provide grace and strength to complete funeral arrangements. Meet financial needs now and in the future. Help the church serve the spiritual and practical needs of this family. Don't let your body of believers fail this test of love.

Deliver all family members from feeling guilty. Show them this tragedy was not their fault. Help them remember they are human; subject to the frailties and limitations of humanity. Put their lives back together, Lord. Fill this deep hole of hurt and pain with your comfort and love. Help each one involved move forward with their life and find joy again.

"For just as the sufferings of Christ flow over into our lives, so also through Christ our comfort overflows." (2 Cor. 1:5)

Prayer for Those Living Together Outside of Marriage

Only Wise God, you gave your Word to keep us happy and holy and in joyful relationship with you and one another. Why won't we ever learn that your ways are for our good? Scores of couples all around me are living together without the benefit of a marriage license. People at work, in neighborhoods, and at colleges ignore your commandments as though they didn't exist and move in together. They forget that you established families to be the foundation of society. Lord, they are tearing down with their own hands the very relationships they want to build. Why don't they remember that your curse and judgment is on them when they sin?

Father of pure love, I know your heart is grieved, because my own heart aches over this problem. Show me how to pray effectively and fervently for these couples. Help me speak the truth in love to them. Convict them, Lord. They are robbing themselves of your best. Take the scales from their eyes; make them hungry to be obedient to your will. Help them understand that their children suffer because they, as parents, walk in error. Give these couples a desire to marry. Hurry them to the altar, Lord. Establish their homes and families in your love and truth so you can pour out blessings upon them. Surround them with healthy marriages. Give them models—examples of godly husbands and wives—who will care enough to teach them the joy of living in your truth. Thank you, Father, amen.

"Marriage should be honored by all, and the marriage bed kept pure, for God will judge the adulterer and all the sexually immoral." (Heb. 13:4)

A Healing Prayer for PTSD Sufferers

Sovereign Lord, you have all power to see into our hearts, minds, and bodies. You know precisely where disease gnaws away at our bones; you see the mental illness and terror that curl around the crevices of our minds, and you have the power to heal.

So I ask for healing for someone with Post Traumatic Stress Disorder. God, help him to cry out to you from his place of desperation; then you will help. Make him willing to cooperate with you and concerned counselors so you can remove the memories that haunt him; the thoughts that draw him into silence and depression. Take away the vivid memories that cause him to relive events best forgotten. Help him when flashbacks confuse him, mixing up his past and present. Rock him in your comforting arms when he feels vulnerable and violated.

Teach him to develop a friendship with you that will enable him to handle relationships with other people. Bring him back to a normal, fulfilling life, Lord. Teach him to laugh again. Restore him. Bless him. Thank you, Lord, amen.

"His divine power has given us everything we need for life and godliness."
(2 Peter 1:3)

Prayer for an Adult Survivor of Sexual Abuse

*H*eavenly Father, how it must tear at your heart when the people you love are victims of Satan's lies. Lord, I come to you begging help for a dear one who believes these horrible lies!

She was sexually abused as a child, Lord. Ugly memories haunt her. Though she understands herself to be an innocent victim, she feels somehow guilty and unclean. Expose the lie, Lord. Teach her she is more valuable than gold to you. She is unable to trust because she views all men through the skewed lens of her past. Expose the lie. Show her that men can be trustworthy. This woman selfishly guards her own interests because she believes no one else will do it. Expose the lie. Show her that she can depend on you to care for her.

Help her recognize Satan's lies. Help her internalize the truth because she has saturated herself with your Word. Help her to focus her thoughts on you, filling her mind with nobility and purity rather than nasty lies.

Call her to open herself to you so you can heal her wounded spirit. Unfold her; pour your love over her and let her feel your purity. Cleanse every crevice of her soul. Grant grace for her to forgive the perpetrator, and in doing so break free of him forever. Then hold her out for all to see; a sparkling jewel in your hand. Thank you, Lord, amen.

"You will be a crown of splendor in the LORD's *hand, a royal diadem in the hand of your God."* (Isa. 62:3)

A Prayer Concerning Infertility

*F*ather God, you are worthy of praise and adulation. I bow before you and offer thanks and gratitude to you for your ongoing love and care. Lord, the plight and frustration of my friend is well known to you. Barrenness is so painful, especially when all around her are happy families. Squeals of small children fill the parks and playgrounds; moms and dads with kid-packs strapped on stroll along sidewalks. My friend notices every pregnant woman.

My friend longs to start a family. She and her husband's love for one another yearns to be expanded to include children. Father, if the time is right, would you bless her with a baby?

She desires your will, Father. Give her peace and contentment through this time of waiting. Help her realize that, as the author of life, you are trustworthy and totally reliable. Give her confidence that you will choose the best for her and her husband, and that when they finally meet you in heaven they will understand everything. In Jesus' name, amen.

"I say to myself, 'The Lord is my portion; therefore I will wait for him.' The Lord is good to those whose hope is in him, to the one who seeks him." (Lam. 3:24–25)

Protect Us from Road Rage

O gracious Father who protects us, I call out to you against the sin of road rage; an evil that endangers travelers on our highways. I beg your forgiveness for a society ranting and raving on streets and freeways; lashing out at complete strangers.

I plead with you to keep my friends and family safe in their cars. Protect them against the fury on our freeways. Give my friends and family wisdom when they cross paths with an angry person. Calm them and enable them to keep their emotions in check. Don't let the people in my range of influence be guilty of uncontrolled anger, but rather fill them with self-control.

Make them considerate as they drive. Give them the grace to overlook the mistakes of others. Make them willing to turn the other cheek by glancing away from an out-of-control person rather than staring them down. Stop them from chasing down an offending car. Keep them from provoking other drivers with angry words and gestures. Help them to want to please you rather than take revenge. Teach them that you see the godly character they exhibit alone in their cars, even if no one else does. In Jesus' name, I ask you to make them peacemakers instead of troublemakers, amen.

"The acts of the sinful nature are obvious: sexual immorality, impurity and debauchery; idolatry and witchcraft; hatred, discord, jealousy, fits of rage, selfish ambition, dissensions, factions and envy; drunkenness, orgies, and the like. I warn you, as I did before, that those who live like this will not inherit the kingdom of God." (Gal. 5:19–21)

Prayer as an Ambulance Passes

*L*ord, I hear the wailing sirens and see the flashing lights of emergency vehicles. Someone's life is in crisis right now. Please meet them at his point of need, and whatever the outcome, bring them closer to you. If they're not saved, turn their hearts to you. If they're wandering child of yours, use this incident to bring them back to your loving arms. If they're living daily in your love, surround them right now with your presence.

Reassure and comfort those involved—the victim, their family and friends, and the rescuers. Keep the rescue workers safe and give them wisdom as they make life-and-death decisions. Guide their minds and strengthen their bodies and spirits.

I know you are in charge of life's circumstances, even when I don't understand them. I praise you that your ways are perfect and that you are love. In Jesus' name, amen.

"As for God, his way is perfect; the word of the Lord *is flawless. He is a shield for all who take refuge in him." (Ps. 18:30)*

A Prayer for Justice

*H*oly God, you are right and just in all you do. I pray that I will never lose sight of that truth. I pray for my friend in prison. I thank you that he has come to salvation in you—the one and only true God. He knows that in your loving mercy you graciously extended yourself to him. Thank you for showing him the way to your grace!

As he spends time in jail, he'll meet people who have committed equal or greater crimes than he, but who are serving less time. Help him not to get caught up in trying to determine justice based on man's proceedings. Help him to focus on you, the Divine Judge, who always is just. Help him to always remember his sins were paid for by your Son Jesus Christ, thereby allowing him to be justified before you.

Lord, help him to not avenge himself, but to leave vengeance up to you and to be merciful to others as you are merciful to him. May he thoughtfully pray for prosecutors that they would seek appropriate consequences for crimes committed, and that judges and juries would make correct decisions. Lord, help him to rest in your justice and mercy. Thank you, Lord. Amen.

"Do not take revenge, my friends, but leave room for God's wrath, for it is written: 'It is mine to avenge; I will repay,' says the Lord." (Rom. 12:19)

A Plea for a Prisoner's Submission to Authority

Sovereign God, I am praying for your own child who is presently serving time in prison for crimes he committed against you and society. I pray specifically that you would help him develop a spirit of submission. You know he, like all of us, has a propensity to rebel and want to do it his way—to be captain of his own ship.

Lord, help him to recognize his natural desires and choose to seek your way and will in his every action. Please help him to recognize those positions of authority you have ordained: the unit management and staff, treatment personnel, and security staff. They are intended for his good.

Help him to be diligent in studying your Word, so that on the occasions when authorities give man-centered advice that is contrary to your counsel, he will be respectful to them and yet resolve to obey you. I pray that he develops such a spirit of genuine submissiveness that he will be a lighthouse for you in his sphere of influence. Thank you for this one that belongs to you, Lord. I speak this prayer in the name of Jesus, amen.

"Submit to one another out of reverence for Christ." (Eph. 5:21)

Gratitude for the Incarceration of a Loved One

*M*erciful Father, I come to you on behalf of one of your own. You know he was living a sin-infested life that was spiraling downward and out of control. He had no time for you or even anything humanly thought to be good. In your providence he went too far and is now behind bars for criminally offending others.

I thank you for stopping him in his tracks, for giving him "think" time. I thank you for graciously reaching into his life and drawing him to yourself.

Obviously, he is a changed person. You know how his inner self has changed. Others are seeing that his outer person is different. As he grows in you, he will become more Christ-like, developing a spirit that is very attractive to others. They will undoubtedly commend him for his behavior, thinking it is a result of self-effort.

Lord, please keep it fresh in his mind that his improvement is not because of his own righteous thoughts and deeds, but because of your love. You looked at his condition and graciously offered him eternity with you. Help him always recognize and acknowledge that it is your righteousness accounted to him that has brought him to where he is. Then whenever others comment, he will boldly point them to you. I thank you, in Jesus' holy name, amen.

"But we also rejoice in our sufferings, because we know that suffering produces perseverance." (Rom. 5:3)

A Plea for Freedom

*L*ord, I pray for my friend in prison. He has few choices. He is told when to get up and go to bed, when to eat, when to exercise, and when to bathe. He is told when to go to school, to work, and to treatment group. He is told when he may have visitors and when he may not. It is confinement 24/7!

Even when he has free time and desires to study your Word, it is a challenge. The sitting areas are noisy with the sounds of television, computer games, and socialization. The dorm is quieter, but the environment sedates him to drowsiness because his body is accustomed to sleeping there.

Life is lived in a few thousand square feet. He is never free from distractions. He never has time alone with his thoughts or alone with you.

He is yearning to be outside the fence, geographically free. Lord, help him to remember that physical freedom is simply freedom of the outer self—his outer self that naturally desires the things of the world.

Lord, you have set him free spiritually. His inner self is yours. Help him to remember he is free to serve you; to be salt and light to those who also struggle within those few thousand square feet. Help him because of the sacrifice Jesus made for him, amen.

"For he who was a slave when he was called by the Lord is the Lord's freedman; similarly, he who was a free man when he was called is Christ's slave." (1 Cor. 7:22)

Walk with This Prisoner as He Is Released from Jail

*M*erciful Father, I thank you for this one who serves you with his whole heart. He needs your help more than ever now, God. Prison drove him to accept you because he had nothing else; no other hope. But on his release he returns to the glittering world that tempted him before. Help him, Lord. Enable him to resist temptation by staying away from his old haunts and his old acquaintances. Let him see the world through your eyes—recognizing evil as evil and finding it disgusting.

Call him to a closer relationship with you than he had while incarcerated. Convict him if he neglects reading his Bible and praying for even one day. Mend broken family relationships. Guide him to a church that will warmly accept and mentor him. Give him strong Christian friends that hold him accountable and inspire him to serve you. Lead him to a job so he can provide for his needs honorably.

Then Lord, as he follows you, pour your blessings over his head and help him to remember to lift his voice in praise and gratitude to you every day. Thank you for your love and mercy. In Jesus' name, amen.

"You, my brothers, were called to be free. But do not use your freedom to indulge the sinful nature; rather, serve one another in love." (Gal. 5:13)

Help Me Care for My Elderly Parents

*L*ord God, you are my strength and my song. How desperately I need you to be that for me and for my aging parents. My folks are becoming more and more feeble by the day. They shake with palsy and struggle to remember the most routine functions of daily life. They have needs that must constantly be met—prescriptions to pick up, doctor appointments to keep, and groceries to buy. Their fears overwhelm them, and they grow more discouraged and frustrated by the day. I know that life will not get easier for them. God of all comfort, be with them.

Precious Lord, I need your grace and patience, too. My own schedule is so demanding; help me fit Mom and Dad's needs into my day without neglecting everything and everyone else. Show me your priorities for this period of my life. Help me not resent their demands on my time. I want to serve them lovingly and generously, as they have served me. Forgive me, Lord, when I feel angry and annoyed. There are days I don't know whether to scream at them or weep with them. It is so hard to watch them deteriorate. Give me compassion; help me model kindness. Father, we have such a few days left together. Help us finish well, supporting and encouraging one another in you. Lord, you've promised I can do all things in your strength. I ask you for help in this trial. Thank you.

"When Jacob had finished giving instructions to his sons, he drew his feet up into the bed, breathed his last and was gathered to his people." (Gen. 49:33)

Prayer When a Parent Has Dementia

*G*od of patience and comfort, here I am again crying out to you for help. My father's life has been destroyed by dementia. He is utterly confused; living in a world beyond my reach, believing things not true, angry and accusing. He does not recognize me anymore; family and friends are strangers to him. He is unable to perform simple daily functions. Frying an egg, balancing his checkbook, even enjoying a ride in the country are too much for him. He wanders from chair, to yard, to his room—endlessly circling all day long. Paranoid, he babbles of enemies who stalk him. I do not recognize the kind, intelligent, loving man who was my father. Where has he gone, Lord? Dad has died, and yet I cannot bury him. O God, help!

How could you let this happen, Lord? He doesn't deserve this terrible disease. I am angry—at you, at him, at me. I can't stand to see him in this state of mental disarray. My heart is broken. This is a living death; an unending grief.

What am I to do, Father? I can't keep him at home. Yet how can I place him in a care facility, betraying the father who met my every need? Lead me through this wilderness; guide my decisions. Help me find kind caregivers who will honor him even in his present state. You are my only Rock of Refuge, Lord. Please come and help me now. Thank you.

"The LORD *is a refuge for the oppressed, a stronghold in times of trouble. . . for you,* LORD, *have never forsaken those who seek you.*" (Ps. 9:9–10)

Prayer for a Friend in a Troubled Marriage

I know that we have talked about this before, Lord. Many times. Still, I bring her to you again. I am like the widow before the judge, refusing to give up because I know that you are in the restoration business. You bring wayward children home. You make peace between races and nations, fathers and sons, pastors and congregations. Why won't you make peace in my friend's marriage?

Father, as tired as I am of praying about it, she is tired of living it. She is tired of hearing about how a marriage should look, when hers only causes pain. She is tired of feeling like a second-class Christian because hers isn't the perfect marriage. And Lord, her pain sometimes causes great doubt of herself and of her faith. Sometimes, Lord, I admit, she even doubts you.

But you are the great reconciler. In Christ, you make peace between men and God. And after all, Lord, what greater division exists than that? So, Lord, I am asking for you to do whatever it takes to bring wholeness to this relationship. Use whatever you need to get this man's attention. Help them both to see what trips them up and how they contribute to their conflict. Help them to identify the enemy as he divides them. Help them to be thankful for what they do have.

Give her hope. Help her believe that change is possible and that you will keep her, meeting her every need, every day, until change comes. May nothing ever shake her love for you. Set her in you like pebbles in concrete . . . for you are the lover of our souls. Amen.

"Heal me, O LORD, and I will be healed; save me and I will be saved, for you are the one I praise. (Jer. 17:14)

Keep a Marriage Together in the Face of Divorce

*H*eavenly Father, couples expect oneness and sharing when they marry, but often they experience pain, anger, and coldness instead.

You designed marriage as an earthly example of the relationship of Christ and the church. This relationship created for mutual love and satisfaction does not develop easily, sometimes not at all. Help couples realize the sacredness of this relationship even as it falls short of the ideal. Place within them the determination to honor their marriage vows and commitment, even when their legitimate needs are not met. Help them turn to you to fill the aching void in their lives. Use this pain to enhance their relationship with you.

Lord, give them intimate times with you as they study your Word and talk with you in prayer. Show them how to love their spouses by praying for them, choosing to act in their best interests, and returning good for evil. Keep them faithful to each other even when the relationship is not personally fulfilling. Help them understand the importance of their marriage in others' lives. Remind them that their marriage is crucial to the healthy development of their children and the stability of the Christian and local communities.

Thank you that you work in people's hearts and that change is possible. Transform faltering marriages into a vibrant relationships that will bring joy to couples and to all those who witness them, in Jesus' name, amen.

"This is a profound mystery—but I am talking about Christ and the church. However, each one of you also must love his wife as he loves himself, and the wife must respect her husband." (Eph. 5:32–33)

A Prayer for the Innocent Partners of Divorce

O God of justice and mercy, I boldly approach you today on behalf of the innocent partners of divorce. I know you identify with them, because you were also an innocent victim of divorce. Jeremiah says the many adulteries of your wife, Israel, left you no choice but to put her away. It broke your heart, God. Your agony echoes through the pages of the Old Testament. That's why you understand the anguish of these victims.

Be with these people when they feel tossed away like a used up plastic cup—when they feel worthless. Help them understand how precious they are to you. Supply energy when they're too tired to finish the day's chores. Let them rest in your hand. Lead them to ask for forgiveness for past mistakes, then assure them you forgive them. Take away any guilt they feel over a divorce they didn't choose.

Be their perfect spouse. Give them wisdom as they prayerfully parent. Provide for them when money runs low. Call them to spend time with you when loneliness hollows out their hearts. Show them clearly that they can be successful—even happy—if they depend on you. Fill them with your joy. In Jesus' name, amen.

"I gave faithless Israel her certificate of divorce and sent her away because of all her adulteries." (Jer. 3:8)

A Cry from an Abandoned Wife

O God, Father of the fatherless, I call out to you for my abandoned children. I cry from my own loneliness. We know my husband's whereabouts, but we never see him. He took a job far away from us and rarely comes to visit.

It's very confusing for me, Lord. He claims he remains faithful to me and doesn't want a divorce, but thoughts that he may be involved with another woman torture me. Reveal the truth to me, Lord. Show me what to do. Give me a constant sense of your presence so I won't feel so alone.

He says he loves the children, but that's not how he acts. He doesn't even send enough support money. My salary barely feeds us; there's little money for extras. I come home from work and have to care for the kids alone. I'm exhausted.

My husband and I are supposed to be a team, God. I need help raising the children. Convict him. Call him to repentance. Refresh his love for us. Bring him home. But if he refuses to come, I know you have promised to be my husband and defender. I am confident you will help us. Thank you, Lord, amen.

"A *father to the fatherless, a defender of widows, is God in his holy dwelling.*" (Ps. 68:5)

Help My Friend Stand up Under Verbal Abuse

O God, anger rises up in me when I hear my friend's husband speak to her so disrespectfully. It isn't right, Lord. Doesn't he realize how he hurts her? Doesn't he understand how worthless he makes her feel? How his cruel words destroy the intimacy between them? Reveal those truths to him, Lord.

Let her turn to you for comfort, knowing that her husband's opinion matters little in comparison to your evaluation of her. Show her that she is more valuable than rubies to you. Be with her through the turmoil of verbal assassination. Encircle her with your arms.

Don't let her retaliate by hurling damaging words back at her husband, even though the temptation to do so can be nearly overwhelming for her. Because you are her strength, help her remain calm when he insults and accuses. Strengthen her to reject his degrading attitudes toward her. Help her communicate effectively; demanding by her demeanor that he treat her with respect. Help her to boldly stand without anger or fear as she faithfully remains in the marriage. Make her the gentle example that causes him to repent and change. Yank up any root of bitterness before it takes hold in her. Reward her with a loving, godly marriage that honors you. In Jesus' name, amen.

"When they hurled their insults at him, he did not retaliate; when he suffered, he made no threats. Instead, he entrusted himself to him who judges justly." (*1Peter 2:23*)

Give Wisdom in a
Physically Abusive Marriage

O God, I can barely fathom a marriage in which a man would strike his wife! It is a great evil, Lord. How could he sink to such depths of degradation?

Give wisdom to his wife. Give her confidence. Help her to know down deep that this is *his* problem. He has no right to harm her, no matter how angry he gets. At the same time, though, reveal specific ways she contributes to his loss of control, and give her a teachable spirit so she can avoid doing those things. Keep her silent, praying in her thoughts when he begins to rant and rave and she wants to scream at the injustice. Teach her that saying anything at that moment endangers her and her children.

Show her if she should separate from him or stay in the marriage. If she stays, show her how and where to seek help. If she chooses to separate, protect her and the children during the separation.

Don't let her leave because she wants a divorce; let her purpose in leaving be to shock him with the consequences of his actions and afford him the opportunity to repent and change.

Bring strong men around him who will hold him accountable. Give the wife courage to wait until the husband is truly healed before they reconcile. Then bring them back together. Enable them to love each other and model a strong marriage for the children. I pray this in Jesus' name, knowing you are able to work the impossible, amen.

"A wife must not separate from her husband. But if she does, she must remain unmarried or else be reconciled to her husband. And a husband must not divorce his wife." (1 Cor. 7:10–11)

Lord, Reconcile
This Married Couple

*M*y God and my Redeemer, there are only three who know precisely what has happened within this marriage—the husband, the wife, and you. Yet one thing I do know, a vow was spoken before you and witnesses, and you did not take that vow lightly. I've wondered how anyone who listens to that vow being taken can hear it as anything but sacred.

The residue of that broken, shattered vow is all around. There are tears, questions, secrets, desperate phone calls, sleeplessness, unsound decisions, uncontrolled outbursts, insinuations, wonderings, accusations, sobbings, and immeasurable pain. O God, help, please help! There is need for that assurance that only you can provide.

In Isaiah 58 you refer to the "repairer of the breach." You are being asked now, Lord, to be that to these who are in need of reconciliation. Have mercy, Father, and light the way out of this dark, deep cavern of futility and heartache. Apply your balm of healing liberally as you straighten the twisted tentacles of this gnarled situation. Lead them back into conformity with their spoken vows and your holy Word. Thank you, Lord, amen.

"If you return to the Almighty, you will be restored. . . . Surely then you will find delight in the Almighty and will lift up your face to God. You will pray to him, and he will hear you, and you will fulfill your vows." (Job 22:23, 26–27)

Prayer for
Children of Divorce

*A*bba Father, you hold a special place in your heart for innocent children. How grieved you must feel as the ranks of "children of divorce" grow larger and larger each year. How your heart must break.

You understand their anguish more than we do. You know when smiles or bad behavior mask searing pain. You recognize wounds that refuse to heal. Do you cry with them, Father? Do you long to comfort them? Do you whisper to them in the night?

Help them to listen for your loving whispers, God. Gently wipe away their tears. When they wonder if they can ever trust again, teach them that you are dependable, trustworthy, and faithful. Give them role models who will live healthy marriages before their eyes, so that by watching those relationships the children can know how to successfully craft their own marriages. Don't let them fear commitment. Assure them that you have bright futures for them.

Surround them with your loving arms, Lord, until they grow into noble Christians who serve you and love their families fervently. I pray this in Jesus' name, amen.

"Jesus said, 'Let the little children come to me, and do not hinder them, for the kingdom of heaven belongs to such as these.'" (Matt. 19:14)

The Prayer of a Wife Forced to Work Outside the Home

*D*ear Lord, I am so frustrated and angry! I want to be able to raise my children, not hand them over to another woman who can't love them the way I do. I want to watch them grow. I want to instill godly values in them. I want to shape them into young adults that love and serve you. Instead, I pick them up every night just in time to rush home, fix dinner, and put them to bed. I barely see them on weekdays.

Lord, I am willing to sacrifice to stay at home with my children. I can live in a smaller house, drive a less expensive car, eat more macaroni and cheese. Please change my husband's heart. I've begged, pleaded, yelled, and cried, but he won't listen. Please make a way where there seems to be no way. Touch his heart; speak to him about our responsibilities as parents.

Help me not to become resentful and bitter about this. Lord, forgive me for lashing out at him in anger. Give me patience until I can be a stay-at-home mom. Help me to cherish every moment I have with my children. I pray for a hedge of protection around them while we're separated each day. Lord, I thank you with all of my heart that your eyes are always upon them. Amen.

"I have learned the secret of being content in any and every situation, whether well fed or hungry, whether living in plenty or in want. I can do everything through Him who gives me strength." (Phil. 4:12–13)

Prayer for a Woman Never Loved by Daddy

aithful Father, who is more important in a little girl's life than her daddy? He is her first love; her idol. She sees herself through his eyes. If he calls her beautiful, she believes she is beautiful. If he adores his little princess, she knows she is a treasure.

Holy God, my friend's father didn't know how to love her. He ignored her, criticized and ridiculed her, and punished her harshly. He didn't know how to cuddle her. He never told her he loved her and he probably never will. That's why she can't feel worthy of love. She exhausts her energies striving to prove she is loveable, still struggling to win Daddy's love. And when she can't, she searches for other loves to fill the father-shaped hole in her heart. But you and I both know that nothing will satisfy her until she recognizes who you are.

Open her eyes to the depth of your love for her. Welcome her to Abba Father, her Daddy God. Beckon her to crawl up on your lap and press her head against your strong Father-chest, sinking into the warmth of your love. Enfold her in your arms. Let your truth envelop her. Breathe your Holy Spirit into her heart—filling the emptiness, healing the wounds. Bend your head to whisper beauty. Assure her she is your treasure, your sparkling diamond, and you accept her just as she is. Teach her to close her eyes and quiet her soul because she recognizes your true identity at last. You are her true Father who offers eternal love. She is your beloved daughter. Through Christ you have made this possible, amen.

"Even if my father and mother abandon me, the Lord *will hold me close."*
(Ps. 27:10 NLT)

Please Help with a
Difficult Roommate

*L*ord, my daughter was so happy to find a roommate. She thought they would enjoy living together. Instead, the environment in my daughter's home is causing her emotional anguish. She's vague about specific problems, Lord, so I don't fully understand the situation. I just know she calls me in tears.

Although it hurts me to see my daughter in pain, part of me thinks this is great practice for a future marriage. So I'm asking you to teach both girls how to honestly communicate ideas and feelings. Help my daughter be willing to really listen to any flaws her roommate points out, even if it is done poorly. Help her to take responsibility for any problems she has caused and work to change.

Encourage her to depend on you to get her through this. Give her wisdom to recognize unjust criticism and the courage to state why she refuses to own it. Teach her to fully and clearly articulate any difficulties she perceives. Help her speak the truth in love, making every effort not to harm her roommate, but knowing that sometimes feelings get hurt in the process of solving problems. Use this to shape my daughter into a strong person who loves you more each day.

If the other girl is as difficult as my daughter thinks, soften her. Lead her to treat my child with kindness and respect. Then when this period of time ends and they are free to separate, help my daughter use this experience as a reminder to take great care in choosing a marriage partner. I praise you, Lord, for painful lessons! Amen.

"Instruct a wise man and he will be wiser still; teach a righteous man and he will add to his learning." (Prov. 9:9)

A Prayer for Women Suffering Guilt after Abortion

*L*ord, you are matchless; Creator of the universe, yet friend to those you have created. I appeal to you, loving Father, on behalf of the many women who have aborted the life of the developing child within them because they saw no better way out of their difficult situations. Take pity on them as they face the grief and agony that plagues them night and day.

Would you cradle them with the warmth of your fatherly embrace each time they wince when they see a woman in maternity clothes; each time they see an infant or hear its cry? When shame floods their soul and they struggle to hold back the bitter tears, would you comfort them? When they replay the decision they made and the pain of it doesn't diminish, Father, beckon them to you. Grant them the relief that comes when they choose to repent and put their sin under the blood of the Savior, Jesus Christ. I ask that these hurting women who carry this pocket of sadness will be drawn to you and will receive your love and forgiveness.

Thank you for the power of the blood of Christ! Isaiah said that though our sins are as scarlet, they shall be white as snow! We are awed at that, Father, yet we know by faith that it is truth. Amen.

"Though your sins are like scarlet, they shall be white as snow; though they are as red as crimson, they shall be like wool." (Isa. 1:18)

Give My Friend
Assurance of Salvation

*D*ear God of new beginnings, I bow before you in gratitude, thankful that you loved my friend enough to pull him from the depths of sin.

Thank you for sending your Son to die for him while he was still a sinner. Thank you for forgiving his sins even though he deserved the death penalty—because the payment for any sin is death. Thank you for claiming him as your own. Thank you for viewing him as righteous through your Son Jesus.

I praise you, Lord, for making him able to believe in you. I thank you that he openly confessed you as his Lord and Savior. I ask that you make him so grateful for your forgiveness and love that he will continue to confess you over and over to people.

Now give him confidence in you, Father. Help him to understand that *everyone* has sinned and fallen short of your glory. Show him that there is no longer any reason for him to feel guilt, because there is *no condemnation* for anyone who belongs to you, and he belongs to you.

Help him to know that even during those times when he may not *feel* saved from hell, he is. Unlike his feelings, your promises stand firm. I thank you, God, that he can boldly approach you through your Son Jesus, amen.

(Scripture references in text: Rom. 5:8; Rom. 6:23; Rom. 10:9; Rom. 3:32; Rom. 8:1)

"*Whoever believes in the Son has eternal life, but whoever rejects the Son will not see life, for God's wrath remains on him.*" (John 3:36)

Help Me Get Along with My Neighbor

*L*ord, this has been such a difficult struggle with my neighbor. It has cost me so much, and I continue to pay a very high price. If I could take back what I said to her as a result of the damage she has done to me, I would. But she will not accept that I am sorry for what I said. She will not allow me to apologize.

You warn us over and over in the Bible to control our tongues because they are desperately wicked. Somehow it seems that I must learn this lesson the hard way! I am so sorry. Please forgive me and help me to accept your discipline in this.

How can my neighbor be so selfish and mean and uncaring of another human being? You say, Lord, that we are to pray for our enemies, and she is my enemy. Sometimes I get so angry, Lord, I almost choke on the words. I say terrible things to you about her, and then I have to repent of my awful attitude.

Lord, give me grace daily to deal with this situation. I get so discouraged and angry. I do pray for her salvation, since I know that is her only hope. Please help me to have the attitudes and feelings you want me to have toward her, for my real love is to please you. Thank you my precious Lord and Savior, amen.

"A man who lacks judgment derides his neighbor, but a man of understanding holds his tongue." (Prov. 11:12)

Prayer Following an Argument

*H*eavenly Father, you know what angry words were spoken today. Some of them were spoken out of frustration rather than truth. Our relationship is tense and strained. We cannot see each other's point of view.

If I am wrong, please show me—even if it is difficult for me. Where I have lost my temper and said harsh words, calm my stirred up emotions. Forgive me for saying things that may have hurt him. Let me be humble enough to apologize for blurting out things I now regret.

If I am right, help me carefully choose my words and present my thoughts in a way that won't make him defensive. Then change his heart.

Lord, please don't allow this issue to put a lasting wedge between us. Break down any walls that cause either of us to refuse to see the truth. Your Word says Satan prowls around like a hungry lion wanting to rip us apart and devour us. I know he loves to see us angry and us at odds with each other. I pray, Lord, that you will not let our relationship be torn apart. Melt us back together in your everlasting love. Restore our hearts to closeness and unity once again. In Jesus' name, amen.

"Therefore, as God's chosen people, holy and dearly loved, clothe yourselves with compassion, kindness, humility, gentleness and patience. Bear with each other and forgive whatever grievances you may have against one another. Forgive as the Lord forgave you." (Col. 3:12–13)

Help During a
Midnight Emergency

*G*od of hope, I come to you during this emergency. You see my friend in the hospital right now, critically ill. O Lord, unless you intervene, I am afraid he will die. Help me know how to pray for him and his family at this difficult time. Father, he is so young, with so much life yet to live; make him well, I pray.

Come as the Great Physician and sit with him; hold him by his right hand, Lord. You alone can heal. You alone can impart strength when all hope is gone. Touch him, heal him, lift him from that bed of sickness, and set him on his feet again, dear Lord. Help him have courage and faith to hang on; to believe that you will make him well. Lord, you healed the sick when you walked the earth. You are unchanging, therefore you can do today what you did in ages past. You are not a respecter of one person above another; you love all equally. I know you love my friend. Come in your love and restore his health.

Wrap your arms around his family. Comfort their hearts, Lord. Help them not give up, no matter what the doctors say. Help them look to you each new day for strength and hope to go on. Show us, his friends, how we can serve them at this difficult time. Thank you, Lord, for giving me faith to believe you hear and answer prayer. I lay my friend in your arms. I trust your will for his life, amen.

"He got up, took his mat and walked out in full view of them all." (Mark 2:12)

Prayer as a Business Fails

*H*igh and lofty God, I bow before you, pleading help for my friend as he declares bankruptcy. He had such high hopes, Lord, but now he is devastated. He staked his reputation and manly pride on the success of his business. He put his whole being into it, determined to make it work.

Lord, it's all gone now and he is broken. How will he support his family? How will he face his business associates? Give him answers. When he feels like a failure, comfort him. Don't let him slump into despair. When he struggles to discover the next step, open doors for him. Help him honestly face mistakes he made so he won't repeat them in the future. Strengthen his business acumen so he can succeed at his next job. Don't let people in his line of work ostracize him. Make him wise as a snake so they will continue to need his skills. Protect him when he attempts to purchase necessary goods and equipment; don't let others discriminate against him financially.

His business was his ministry, Lord. Give him a new way to serve you. Lead him to use this waiting time to mend relationships in his family; let them comfort each other. And Lord, as a nice surprise, could you show him how to actually *enjoy* living without credit? I ask these things in Jesus' name, amen.

"Therefore be as shrewd as snakes and as innocent as doves." (Matt. 10:16)

Help Me Trust When
My Loved One Is Late

*H*eavenly Father, I'm worried. Where is my dear one? Why has she not returned home or even phoned? She is never, ever late, Lord. Is she all right? Is she safe? Quiet my fears, God. I'm concerned there has been an accident.

Help me know how to pray right now. Surround and protect my loved one this moment. Keep her out of harm's way. Customize your help to her. Provide help if the car is stuck beside the road. Send someone safe to meet her every need, even to change a tire. You are with us at all times. Be in this situation as counselor and instructor. Whatever the problem might be, Lord, I'm believing you will solve it.

God, quiet my pounding heart, my wild imagination. Remind her to call home on the cell phone. Or have someone else make a call if her phone isn't working. Bring her home safely, Lord. I'm counting on your protection and care, amen.

"We wait in hope for the LORD; he is our help and our shield." (Ps. 33:20)

Bring Back My Runaway Child

*L*iving God, who knows the heart and mind and will of every person, help me. You see me, Lord, agonized, weeping day and night, and unable to find my runaway child. You know where she is right now. Your eye is upon her. Lord, you alone can help her. You alone can thoroughly search the streets and alleyways, speak her name, and call her home to us. Father, restore this child to our family. Bring this wayward one back into our arms.

Keep her safe on the streets. Let no evil overtake her, Lord. You know she doesn't make wise decisions. Walk with her as she wanders in the night. Lead her to a place of safety. Surround this rebellious child with people who will reach out and help her. Give her a safe place to sleep. Provide food, but make her miserable enough that she yearns for the safety and love of our home again. Cause her thoughts to be drawn to those who love her. Convince her of my love, Lord.

Father, right this moment, speak to my daughter. Fill her with a desire to phone home, or cause her to share her heart with someone who will contact me. Thank you, Lord, for hearing me when I cry out to you. I know you will answer, for you are a loving heavenly Father. In Christ's name, amen.

"If you believe, you will receive whatever you ask for in prayer." (Matt. 21:22)

Prayer for One in Bondage
to Eating Disorders

*F*ather God, I pray to you in hope for this precious young woman who is struggling with an eating disorder. You see her pain. She attempts to conform to the world's image of beauty by starving herself of nourishment. She strives for perfection and feels like a failure when she falls short. You alone know the deceptions that fill her mind and spirit. Minister to her, Lord. Heal her. Touch her with your healing hand.

I am terrified. Spare the life of this one I love. She is destroying her health—ruining with her own hand the beauty you gave her. Indwell her mind, Spirit of Truth, and replace the lies. Help her choose truth, for that is health. Take her hand and pull her from this pit of despair. You love her, and you created her for fellowship with yourself.

Surround this girl with doctors, dieticians, and spiritual advisors. Help her step out of this lifestyle built on false precepts. Show those of us who love her most how to help her. Mobilize us, Great Physician. Use us to lead her out of this death mindset into life and joy again.

Heal our whole family, Lord. Change us where we have contributed to this problem. We desire to glorify and serve you with our lives, amen.

"The LORD is a refuge for the oppressed, a stronghold in times of trouble. Those who know your Name will trust in you, for you, LORD, have never forsaken those who seek you." (Ps. 9:9–10)

Prayer for My Drug-Addicted Child

O my God, you see my son, caught in drug addiction, unable to get free. He has walked in so much horror because of his consuming need for drugs. He is alienated from all who love him. He lives in poverty—dirty and alone. Drugs are killing him, Lord. Help him! He is wasting away, surrounded by addicts and alcoholics and vagrants. His health is ruined; his friends and future are gone. Evil surrounds him on every side. Men and women use him for their own carnal purposes. God, I fear for his life. I'm afraid he'll die in some dark alley, and I will never see him again.

Help him, Father. Our family is broken and suffering. You alone can reach my son in the depth of his need. You alone can find him and restore him to me. Nothing is too hard for you to do. Even this is easy for you because you have all power and all mercy. Reach out and pull my boy back from the gates of hell. Save him, Lord.

Search him out at this moment. Restore to him a sound mind and a pure heart. You are my only hope, Lord. I know you hear me when I call. I trust you to answer this prayer. Thank you, Father, for your faithfulness. Through Christ I pray, amen.

"He sent forth his word and healed them; he rescued them from the grave." (Ps 107:20)

Prayer for Calm after Cancer Diagnosis

*H*eavenly Father, my friend was diagnosed with cancer today. Her voice quivered with fear as she told me the devastating news.

Lord, embrace my friend with the comfort of your presence. She is embarking on a painful and scary journey. Please light the way before her. Help her to sort through the avalanche of feelings churning inside her: shock, disbelief, anger, sadness, and dread. Quell her waves of panic. Give my friend strength and courage to battle the insidious disease attacking her body. Guide her through the maze of medical jargon and therapy options. Sustain her as she endures treatments whose side effects rival the ravages wrought by the cancer.

Thank you that our frail earthly bodies are just temporary dwellings. Calm my friend with your promises of eternal glory. Grant her your perfect peace which transcends all understanding. In Jesus' name I pray, amen.

"Fear not, for I have redeemed you; I have summoned you by name; you are mine. When you pass through the waters, I will be with you; and when you pass through the rivers, they will not sweep over you. When you walk through the fire you will not be burned; the flames will not set you ablaze." (Isa. 43:1–2)

"Now we know that if the earthly tent we live in is destroyed, we have a building from God, an eternal house in heaven, not built by human hands." (2 Cor. 5:1)

A Prayer for Someone in Extreme Danger

*P*recious Lord, I am feeling that your child is in extreme danger. Help me know how to pray for that person right now. Give me insight and knowledge of his particular need as I wait before you. Don't let me pray from my mind or my understanding, Lord. Don't let me just formulate prayers out of my thoughts and desires. Instead, give me your mind and your perspective of his need at this moment; let me pray your heart for him. I believe you can do that, Father.

Lord, stand beside him in this dangerous situation and deliver him—even as your angels stood with Daniel in the lions' den and delivered him. O God, put a wall of safety around your needy child, and do not let danger or evil penetrate that wall and harm him.

Come alongside; lift the one I'm praying for out of danger and out of harm's way. Preserve his life, Lord. Surround him with your peace and your presence. Send appropriate help even as I pray. Blanket this one with love and power and a sound mind. Quiet him; help him focus. Help him know how to help himself. Cause this one to place his trust in you so that you can prove yourself mighty on his behalf. Thank you, Lord, for hearing and helping. Through Christ I pray, amen.

"The angel of the LORD *encamps around those who fear him, and he delivers them."* (Ps. 34:7)

God, It's a Heart Attack!

Prince of Peace, I'm so afraid. He's suffered a heart attack! Get him to the hospital in time. Let there be no long-term damage, Lord. Surround him with the medical help he needs. Whatever the situation is, meet that need. Show each caregiver exactly what to do. Let no time be wasted before he is diagnosed and treated.

Great Physician, be with him. Direct every procedure, whether it is angioplasty, surgery, or another medical intervention. Calm his anxious fears and help him relax and cooperate with those who are trying to help him. Get the family to his side. Send someone to sit with him until his loved ones arrive. Don't let him die, Lord. There is so much yet to share. There are so many conversations that still must take place and so many important memories yet to be made.

I pray against depression and discouragement in him and in the family. Help him accept the diagnosis. Give him courage to reassess his life and make adjustments. Let this be a wake-up call, Father, to appreciate each sunrise and each relationship. Help him get his life in order and daily communicate love and appreciation to his family and friends. If he is not prepared to die, I pray he will acknowledge you as Savior and Lord and settle the question of where he will spend eternity. Thank you for answering my prayer, Lord. Amen.

"My flesh and my heart shall fail, but God is the strength of my heart and my portion forever." (Ps. 73:26)

Help a Person
Threatening Suicide

*A*bba Father, I understand this one threatening suicide. I've been through times of hopelessness when the enemy tricked me into wondering if death might be a welcome escape. But I know it isn't, Lord. Show this depressed person that though life is difficult for everyone, you are with us all and will him help him through this. You can use hard times to shape him into your image. Beckon him to sink into your arms and soak up your comfort.

Lord, if a chemical problem is causing him to think bizarre, sad thoughts, direct him to a doctor who understands and can help with medicine. If his thoughts are confused because he has made wrong choices or views life through a skewed lens, bring a pastor or counselor with wisdom across his path.

If his troubles are actually unendurable, help him lift his eyes to you and remember you never give us more than we can handle. You will provide a way of escape; you will offer relief. Bring friends around him who know how to comfort and support him and won't ignore his cries for help. Give him extra strength to get through this.

Then remind him that tomorrow will be brighter. In Jesus' name, amen.

"I lift up my eyes to the hills—where does my help come from? My help comes from the LORD, the Maker of heaven and earth." (Ps. 121:1–2)

Prayer for a Deceived Loved One

ather, this one I love is deceived. Piece by piece she has created a dream world—full of lies and half-truths—a world all her own. This handmade world has encased her like an eggshell, keeping her safe, yet isolated. Fragile at first with many weaknesses, she has stayed busy adding layers, to make it stronger and thicker. Nothing I say is getting through anymore, Lord. Her shell looks completely impenetrable to me. I have almost given up hope.

As the queen of human reasoning, she shouts me down when I talk, denying the truth that screams at her from her own mirror. She defends herself by explaining away her sin. She says I don't understand and that I don't love her. But I do, Lord.

On our own, we are without hope. And unless you do something, her path will bring her to utter destruction. But you are a God who cracks shells. You speak, and walls fall down. You take action, and the plains are filled with the bodies of those who seek to harm your children. Your Word shatters the human heart, bringing light into darkness. You are the light, and darkness flees from you.

I am begging, Lord. I am asking you to shatter the shell she trusts to protect her. Bring light into her dark world. Offer truth for her lies. Give her no place to hide from your laser-like Holy Spirit. Let her see that her only hope lies in you. Let her trust your love enough to climb out of the shell. Set this one I love free to be wholly yours, to love and serve you all the rest of her life. Because of Jesus, amen.

"Hear my prayer, O God; listen to the words of my mouth." (Ps. 54:2)

A Prayer for Someone with a Sex Addiction

*P*atient Father, strip away the selfishness, denial, and deceit that guard this stronghold in the heart of my friend. Give him courage to confess his secret life and face the realities of his choice to use sex to cope with life's pain. Surround him with people who will honestly confront him, empathetically understand him, boldly walk beside him, and gently restore him.

Reveal to him the power of your unconditional love that reaches beyond his shame and is a lifeline to him in the midst of his struggle. He needs to realize that though you know the rancid details of his sin you still love him. Show him you are faithful and able to meet all of his needs. Help him see that his struggle is not really with sex, but with the faulty way he views himself and the world.

Pick him up when he falters and fails. Give him strength to press on when he feels like giving up. Comfort him in times of depression. Teach him to rely on you for strength. Renew him as he presses on toward recovery. Show him that your plan for him is not just to survive this addiction, but for him to have a transformed and victorious life. Break the cycles and curses of addiction in this family line and bring blessing on generation upon generation with the broken spirit of my friend. I pray through Jesus, amen.

"Then I acknowledged my sin to you and did not cover up my iniquity. I said, 'I will confess my transgressions to the LORD'—and you forgave the guilt of my sin. Therefore let everyone who is godly pray to you while you may be found; surely when the mighty waters rise, they will not reach him.'" (Ps. 32:5–6)

A Prayer for Release from the Prison of Selfishness

*M*erciful Lord, release each of us from the confining bars of the hyphenated self: self-love, self-reliance, self-esteem, self-actualization, self-gratification, self-realization, self-determination, self-assurance, self-indulgence, self-sufficiency, self-will, and self-centeredness.

This prison wears us down, serving number one and promoting our uniqueness. Self-service is the ultimate solitary confinement.

Lord, thank you for entering our lives to deliver us from selfishness. Though our inner self is yours, our outer self persists in the old ways. Though sin still resides in the outer self, thanks to you, it need not reign.

Help us to practice self-control by allowing your Spirit to control us, Lord. Help us to develop genuine humility, and to do nothing out of selfish ambition and vain conceit, but to look to the interests of others. Heavenly Father, we are tired of being instruments of unrighteousness—self-righteousness. We want to be instruments of righteousness—your righteousness. Help us in Jesus' name, amen.

"Therefore do not let sin reign in your mortal body so that you obey its evil desires." (Rom. 6:12)

God, Save My Homosexual Child

O God who sanctifies and delivers, help me! My child has chosen a homosexual lifestyle. She believes this is who she really is. She says she feels happiest with women; more fulfilled with women than men. God, everything in me screams, "No!" and I want to yell. I want to beat on something!

Lord, I hate this sin—this offense against her person and you. She's walked away from all she's believed about you and your Word. She's walked away from those who love her most. Help me cope, Lord. Give me the will and grace to continue to reach out to her in love. Show me how to touch her spirit with truth. God, destroy the defenses she's built. Penetrate her mind. Expose the lies and deception of this lifestyle to her. Convince her again that your Word is truth. Heal her wounded spirit; uproot the enemy.

Lord, help me focus on her need and not on my own. Your Word says you rescue the children of those who love and obey you. Rescue my child. Forgive her sin. Fill her with a spirit of repentance. Draw her back into your arms and into mine. I need a miracle, God. You are all power and all mercy. Save her soul. Please help me, amen.

"I have seen his ways, but I will heal him; I will guide him and restore comfort to him, creating praise on the lips of the mourners in Israel. 'Peace, Peace, to those far and near,' says the Lord. *'And I will heal them.'"* (Isa. 57:18–19)

Prayer for an Alcoholic

*G*reat Jehovah-Ropheka, the Lord, your Healer, you alone can heal this alcoholic I love, and his fractured family. You have seen all the times he has turned to alcohol as an answer to his needs. It has never answered one need, Lord. With each swallow, alcohol has wrapped itself around his mind and spirit more and more. How has this happened, God? His life started with so much promise, so many dreams, and so much hope. Now it seems to be nothing but ruin.

I feel so cheated; so angry and guilty. I feel ashamed, yet the problem isn't mine; it's his. God, I've tried every way I know to help him, but nothing works. The family has become more dysfunctional with every passing day.

Lord, unless you enter his spirit, his mind, and his very soul, he will never be free. Only you can heal the deep wound at the core of his being. Only you can lead him into wholeness. I believe it's your will to heal him, Lord. Rescue him; rescue each one involved. I trust you to meet this need. You've promised that if I cry to you, you would hear me and give me answers. I am watching for your answers, Lord. I am trusting you, amen.

"And I will do whatever you ask in my name, so that the Son may bring glory to the Father. You may ask me for anything in my name, and I will do it." (John 14:13–14)

God, Deliver Your People from the Occult

*D*ear God, who daily lights our path, come and shine upon the peoples of the world once more with your truth. Many in our country and around the globe are serving the false gods of the occult. Millions are pursuing horoscopes, astrology, familiar spirits, and witchcraft as the god of their choice. Others dabble in sorcery and magic and fortune telling. These idolaters knew you once, but were unwilling to glorify you as God. Now, because of wrong choices, their thinking has become futile, and their hearts have grown dark and sinful. They are becoming more and more tangled in this web of death. O Father of mercies, I cry to you on their behalf. Take the scales from their eyes; come and save them. Turn their hearts and minds back to you. Convict their spirits to repent so they might live and not die.

Your commands regarding evil are clearly seen in your Word. How you hate idolatry! You know it leads to death and eternal separation from you. You cannot look at evil, Lord. You have said if we regard iniquity in our hearts, you will not hear us.

Empower your church with love, Lord. Send us forth to wrestle with the powers of darkness until we have freed all who are caught in this bondage. Nothing is too difficult for you, Father God. Help us as we war for the souls of men and women. Then, when victory comes, we will give you praise and glory and lay these trophies of grace at your feet as a testimony to your love and forgiveness. Through Christ, amen.

"Be holy because I, the LORD your God, am holy." (Lev. 19:2)

A Prayer for Release from Haunting Memories

*D*ear heavenly Father, I stand in prayer for your people who are haunted by memories that terrify or accuse them. Your enemy, Satan, is the perpetrator of this evil. Twisted and ugly, he roams this world mentally torturing innocent, forgiven people. He is a liar; the father of all lies. I pray in the powerful name of Jesus who defeated him on the cross. I pray because Jesus loves his sheep and wishes to heal them.

Even though you've forgiven your children, the terrible memories return. Flashbacks of violent events plague some of them. Others can't erase memories of childhood sexual abuse. Millions of women can't forget aborted babies. For others, the specter of youthful sins pops up.

Each time the memories appear unbidden, your children feel anguish. They suffer unbearable guilt and shame, Lord, though some of them were always guiltless. They feel unclean even though they are forgiven. The guilt is Satan's lie. They need your help, holy God. Remind them that as soon as they turned to you, you forgave their sins. You made them new; you cleansed them.

When the memories flash before them, teach them to lift grateful hearts to you, affirming that they are forgiven and that there is no condemnation for them, because they belong to Christ Jesus. Help them firmly fix their thoughts on you and leave no space for Satan. Help them believe they are righteous through your Son Jesus, amen.

"Submit yourselves, then, to God. Resist the devil, and he will flee from you." (James 4:7)

Watch Over and Rescue a Kidnapped Child

O God, this monumental evil seems more than I can bear. How can I live through this? What is happening to the darling child we love more than life? Is she dead? Or worse, is a madman inflicting horrors on her that I dare not imagine? God, I can't bear to think about it. It tortures me. I want to gulp down sedatives and sleep. But I can't—I won't—because she needs me to pray. I believe that my prayers release the power of your mighty arm to help her, to save her, even though it is invisible to me. So show me how to pray!

Protect her, Lord. Rescue her. Grant wisdom to her, show her ways to escape, and then send her rushing to safety. Bring her home safely; unharmed. If she has to endure pain and abuse until then, keep her spirit safe; let her stay normal. Erase any feelings of guilt she might have. Replace fearful thoughts and memories with images of your mighty angels. Your Word says they are surrounding her right now, Lord. Guide her to focus on scripture and on you. Help her to feel a strong sense of your presence through her suffering.

But if she is no longer alive, could you let us know for certain so we can have closure? If she is in heaven with you, Lord, hold her tightly for me, and whisper that I'll see her soon. Then give us a continuing vivid picture of her in your arms . . . happy and content. Thank you, Lord. I am so grateful you love her even more than I do, amen.

"See that you do not look down on one of these little ones. For I tell you that their angels in heaven always see the face of my Father in heaven." (Matt. 18:10)

Prayer for the Family of a Murdered Child

*A*bba Father, I groan in agony and grief with the family of this precious murdered child. What kind of grotesque being perpetrates this kind of evil? I scream against him! I want this demon caught and punished; I want him rendered helpless, unable to kill again.

Help me, Lord, to quiet my churning emotions and to turn all revenge over to the authorities, thankful you have appointed them to exact justice. I ask you to enable the family to turn their burning desire for retribution over to you, knowing that is the first step toward forgiveness—probably the only one they can take right now. Give them confidence you will repay this man for his atrocities. Assure them you don't ever want them to excuse his malevolent actions, just to lay their hatred at your feet so it won't tear at their spirits and destroy them.

Help them welcome the deep grief instead of shutting themselves off from it, because it stands as a testimony to the immeasurable value of their darling child. Walk through sorrow with them, comfort them, and heal them. Assure them that because you lived in their child's heart and they love you, too, they will see their beloved once again in heaven. Let that glorious hope fill them with comfort.

"'It is mine to avenge; I will repay,' says the Lord." (Rom. 12:19)

"Let heaven fill your thoughts. Do not think only about things down here on earth." (Col. 3:2 NLT)

Prayer When Someone Accidentally Kills Another

*G*racious Father, what is more painful than bearing responsibility for the death of another human being? Murderers deserve to suffer, Lord, but we ask for relief and comfort for everyone involved in accidental killings. Pour your love over them.

If carelessness contributed to the accident, God, let the person who was the instrument of the death ask for, and receive, forgiveness. Help him repent of his negligence and change his ways. If he is blameless and the case goes to court, grant justice. Prevent accusers from surrounding and pointing at him, Lord. Let him see your truth that he need not wallow in guilt. Draw him closer to you through this terrible thing. Let this one life-changing event catapult him toward godliness.

Remind him to pray daily for the grieving family and, if the day comes when the family contacts him, provide the right words for him to speak, so that instead of increasing their pain, he will soothe it.

Help the family of the victim through this tragedy. Encamp around them. Cover them with your wings; cradle them in your nest of comfort. Help them to forgive, so that resentfulness and anger won't destroy their spirits. We know you can heal and work good in the midst of this, Father. Please do it. We ask in your Son Jesus' name, amen.

"And what I have forgiven him—if there was anything to forgive—I have forgiven in the sight of Christ for your sake, in order that Satan might not outwit us." (2 Cor. 2:10–11 NLT*)*

Prayer for a Relationship Broken by Adultery

*F*aithful and true God, I am heartsick. My husband has slept with another woman. I am angry and disappointed. I feel used and abandoned and betrayed. I am furious he has cast our wedding vows aside and destroyed our life together with this selfish, thoughtless act. Hatred for him is choking out my love; I can't think or function. I want to lock him out of my life and my house. I don't want to deal with this, yet I know I must.

Help me know what to do. We've invested years in our marriage and our children, Lord. Our family, our finances, and our future will be ruined if we divorce. Help me not act rashly. Lead me to wise, godly counsel. Show me the way.

Lord, turn my husband's heart back to me and the children. Bring him home. Help us get the help we need to begin again. Show me how I need to change if I have contributed to our marriage problems. Help us rebuild on your strong foundation. Enable me to forgive him and forget this heartache. Make me willing to work for the restoration of our marriage. Help him receive your forgiveness, Lord, and enable him to live righteously. Thank you for hearing my prayer, amen.

"Once you were alienated from God and were enemies in your minds because of your evil behavior. But now he has reconciled you." (Col. 1:21–22)

A Prayer on the Death of an Unsaved Loved One

O God, my loved one is dead. And I don't think she's saved. My soul cries out in agony. I don't want her to be separated from you for eternity. I want to see her again; to rejoice with her in heaven.

Lord, I know you love each person you create. You love us enough to let us accept or reject your love. You sent your beloved Son to die so we could choose you, but I don't know if she chose you.

Your Word says you are not willing that any should perish. I cling to the hope that in the final moments of her life, she said, "I choose you, Lord. I choose to live forever and ever."

I submit to your loving sovereignty and your all-wise plans for my life and hers. I pray in the name of the Savior of the world, amen.

"The Lord is not slow in keeping his promise, as some understand slowness. He is patient with you, not wanting anyone to perish, but everyone to come to repentance." (2 Peter 3:9)

A Prayer for
One with Diabetes

*G*racious Father, this one you love is afflicted with diabetes, a disease that can cause damage in every organ of the body. Help him, Lord. Keep him from denial. Give him a keen awareness of the seriousness of this illness that can cause eventual blindness or amputation. Through his own wise actions, help him to partner with you in protecting his body. Inspire him to do exercise that will help regulate his insulin naturally. Give him the strength to eat wisely.

Don't let diabetes dominate his life and thoughts. Give him a grateful attitude, thankful for modern medicine that enables him to keep this dangerous disease under control. Lead him to the right doctor and give the doctor wisdom in the treatment he recommends.

Cause my friend to take responsibility for his own body, diligently monitoring his own glucose levels and regulating his blood sugar properly. If he becomes ill, keep his insulin from raging out of control. If he injures himself, allow his body to heal quickly. Keep his circulatory system healthy and help him avoid infection.

Don't let diabetes be his identity. Don't let it shorten his life or curtail his daily work. Don't let it conquer him. Instead, make him victorious through you. Amen.

"No, in all these things we are more than conquerors through him who loved us." (Rom. 8:37)

A Prayer for a Woman Suffering from Breast Cancer

*H*eavenly Father, the cancer every woman fears has attacked my friend. This dreaded disease has become her constant companion. It drains her energy, confuses her thoughts, and taunts her as she tucks her children into bed at night, seeps into her dreams. She is terrified she will die and leave her husband and children. Wipe away that fear and replace it with trust in you.

She is afraid of disappointing her husband, of losing him. She has lost the part of her body he found most alluring. She fears he will no longer find her beautiful and she won't have the energy to meet his needs. Deepen her husband's love for her and help him communicate his feelings in ways she can understand. Enable her to believe she is still beautiful to him. Strengthen their marriage. Show her that her beauty never came from a perfect body, but from your Spirit shining through her.

Don't allow the cancer to dominate her life. Instead, teach her to submit her future to you. Let her feel your unconditional love and acceptance. Draw her close. Envelop her in your peace and comfort. Give her strength when she feels nauseated. Keep her from feeling guilty when she is too tired to get up off the couch. Send people to her who will help care for the children and prepare food. Meet any financial needs that arise.

Illuminate a Bible promise that will sustain her through this difficult time. Banish the cancer, Lord. Heal her totally and completely. Cause renewed energy to surge through her body. Grant her a long, full life of service to her family and you. In Christ's name, amen.

"But for you who revere my name, the sun of righteousness will rise with healing in his wings. And you will go out and leap like calves released from the stall." (Mal. 4:2)

A Prayer for a Man with Prostate Cancer

Dear Lord, my friend with prostate cancer is so afraid. To him, this seems like the worst tragedy that could have struck. It threatens his manhood. He fears impotence and worries how his wife will feel toward him if he can no longer perform sexually. Insecurity sweeps over him in waves. Reveal to him that his identity is not in his sexual prowess. Don't let the enemy cancer come between this married couple, Lord, but draw them closer together. Show his wife how to reassure him that she loves him for so many things other than the intimate side of their relationship. Help her list the ways she appreciates him. Give her comforting words to speak even though she, too, is afraid. Help him comfort her in return. Beckon them both to turn their fears over to you and rest in your peace, which transcends understanding.

Call them to lift their voices in praise and gratitude for early diagnosis and modern medicine. Help them look to you for wisdom as they research the best treatment options. Please don't allow fear to influence their decision, instead point them to your answers for the right treatment. When they finally decide what they want to do, and the doctors commence with the procedure, build a wall of protection around him. Let nothing go wrong. Keep all side effects and infections at bay and send your healing spirit flowing through every part of his body. Heal him completely, Lord. Give him a long life of ministry dedicated to you. In Jesus' name, amen.

"And the peace of God, which transcends all understanding, will guard your hearts and your minds in Christ Jesus." (Phil. 4:7)

A Prayer for Someone in Chronic Pain

erciful Father, I come to you on behalf of my friend who suffers from chronic pain. It has commandeered her whole life. It dogs her waking hours; it stalks her sleep at night; it robs her of enjoyment when she spends time with others. It isolates her from family and friends who have never experienced pain and can't identify with it. She feels desperate. Hopelessness hovers over her like thick fog. She wonders how she can live through more years of this, afraid the pain will continue to increase until she can no longer endure it. Show her you won't give her more than she can bear. Help her believe your promise. Enfold her in your arms during the long, dark hours. Guide her to focus her thoughts on you and your Word. Ease her pain. Make it bearable.

Show yourself strong on her behalf, Lord. Clothe her with your courage; give her supernatural strength to endure. Arm her with wisdom to understand that pain and lack of sleep drain energy. Banish any feelings of guilt and uselessness when she can't do as much as she once could. Surround her with your love during times of disillusionment when she questions why you would allow this in her life. Don't let pain shake her faith. Strengthen her when she thinks she can't live through it. Put her in touch with techniques of pain management that will work for her. Teach her to praise you through her pain. Then heal her, Lord. In Jesus' powerful name, amen.

"I will praise the LORD, who counsels me; even at night my heart instructs me. I have set the LORD always before me. Because he is at my right hand, I will not be shaken." (Ps. 16:7–8)

A Prayer for Headache Sufferers

*D*ear Jesus, my friend's excruciating headaches are the invisible enemy that seems to consume her entire life. She lives in fear that one could strike at any time. When they do come, she barely manage to drag herself out of bed, but she is expected to continue life as usual. She has to cook, clean the house, care for the kids, and go to work. It is overwhelming for her, Lord. She feels as though she can't do it. To add to the problem, no one understands—she doesn't look any different than usual. Suffering in silence, she feels lonely.

Please help her, Lord. When the headaches strike, help her relax rather than bunching up with the fear and stress that exacerbate her pain. Send her to a doctor who will understand and work hard to figure out what to do for her. Help him find the underlying causes of her problem. Guide him to the right medications. Give her friends who are sensitive to her and able to recognize when she is hurting. Make them people of prayer, who will call out to you, and also help in practical ways when she can't function.

Lead her to take responsibility for her own body by continuing to search for recent medical developments that might help. Teach her how to eat and exercise in ways that will diminish the number and intensity of her headaches. Teach her to raise her heart in gratitude to you that this illness is not life threatening. And in the times when the pain strikes, draw her closer to you, showing her how to rest in your love. In Jesus' name, amen.

"I pray that out of his glorious riches he may strengthen you with power through his Spirit in your inner being." (Eph. 3:16)

A Prayer for One with a Debilitating Illness

*O*Father, it's impossible for me to comprehend why you would allow such a horrible disease in the life of this one I love. Why her, Lord? Why? I know she wonders. I see longing for a normal life in her eyes; I hear it in the slurred words I strain to follow. I've seen the holes her elbows poke into the drywall when she falls. I know she wants to taste real food instead of taking her nourishment through a tube. The signs of depression show in her face, and my heart twists into knots, mirroring her hands. I know that you didn't cause the illness; evil never comes from you. But I know you could heal her. Why have you chosen not to? It breaks my heart to watch her slide toward death.

Yet her spirit amazes me—the way she accepts caregiving without complaint. I remember when she first became ill. She wasn't so sweet then, Lord, but you used her trials to make her more like you. You've formed her character into a treasure more precious than gold.

Continue to comfort and sustain her, God. Help her to remain calm when pain increases. Every time she feels useless, assure her that her self-worth doesn't come from what she can do but from her value to you. Keep her eyes on you through this living death. Give her courage and hope as she faces the inevitable. Fix her thoughts on heaven. And help those of us who love her to enjoy every second she has left on this earth, knowing we will see her again someday. In Jesus' name, amen.

"These have come so that your faith—of greater worth than gold, which perishes even though refined by fire—may be proved genuine and may result in praise, glory and honor when Christ Jesus is revealed." (2 Pet. 1:7)

A Prayer for a Paraplegic

*O*God, show me how to pray for this one whose trials I can't begin to comprehend or understand. I am able to walk to the bathroom and close the door alone—he is trapped in a wheelchair and needs someone else to wipe his bottom and lift him into bed. His dreams lay broken around him. Many of his relationships have evaporated. The life he expected will never be. Yet his face glows with a nobility that can come only from you; his uncomplaining spirit shames me and points me to you. I thank you for him.

Give him the best, Lord. As you did for Job, replace his lost blessings with even greater ones. Fill his lonely hours with companions who love him. Send caregivers who will get great joy from meeting his needs, people who know how to remain invisible when he wants privacy, but will offer warmth and conversation when he needs love. Open your coffers to provide the food aids and medical supplies he needs.

If he blames himself because his own foolishness caused the accident that crippled him, teach him to accept your forgiveness and live without guilt. Infuse him with a "can do" attitude. Replace his old dreams with new ones. Open his eyes to recognize new ways to use his mind and talents. Call him to make you the focus of his life. Instruct him in prayer, training him as a mighty warrior in spiritual realms. Make him victorious through Jesus' name, amen.

"But our citizenship is in heaven. And we eagerly await a Savior from there, the Lord Jesus Christ, who, by the power that enables him to bring everything under his control, will transform our lowly bodies so that they will be like his glorious body." (Phil. 3:20–21)

A Prayer for a Mentally Challenged Person

Gracious and merciful Father, thank you for this gentle, mentally challenged man. His deep relationship with you has touched so many lives. Thank you for the simple, loving way he views life, for the complete assurance you have given him of your love and salvation. Drive all feelings of inadequacy and worthlessness far from this dear man. Reveal to him that you have a purpose for his life. Enable him to forgive the people around him who feel superior and ridicule him openly because they don't understand him. Heal the pain they inflict. Calm him when he feels frustrated at his inability to cope with the problems of every day life. Lead him to bring his fears to you and trust you to care for him. Call him to turn to you when he feels lonely. Draw him closer to you and strengthen his character through the difficulties he encounters daily. Communicate to him how much you delight in him.

Make his ways pleasing in your sight. Give his parents confidence that you will provide for his future by giving him favor with the people he meets. Send lifelong friends across his path who will view him as you do. Open their eyes to the many ways he enriches their lives. Give those friends the opportunity to grow more unselfish and more like you as they minister to him. Teach them to cherish him more as the years glide past. In Jesus' name, amen.

" When a man's ways are pleasing to the LORD, he makes even his enemies live at peace with him." (Prov. 16:7)

A Prayer Near the End
of a Terminal Illness

*O*mniscient Father, it is difficult to understand why my dear friend has to die before he has had a chance to live to old age. So many of us have prayed in faith, asking you to touch him. We know you can make him well if you so choose.

My friend clings to hope as he prays for his own healing, though it appears you have decided to answer with a no. Help him to accept your will for his life, Father. Show him that you decided the length of his days before he was born, and you will leave him here until your purpose for his life is complete. Fill him with peace about his family as he stares death in the face. Enable him to open his hands and entrust his loved ones' future to your care.

Give him the right words to say to family and friends. If he needs to express his preferences for dealing with extraordinary medical measures toward the end, help him communicate his wishes clearly. If he should discuss his will and make funeral arrangements, give him wisdom and courage to do that. If any rift divides the family, show him how to address those so you can mend them. Don't let anything be left unsaid or unforgiven. Let affirmations of his love flow from him to comfort the ones he loves. Show them how to speak love and release to him in return. Give them all peace. Fill their thoughts and words with joy because of the hope and assurance that they will be reunited in heaven. Use his last days on earth to glorify you. In Jesus' name we pray, amen.

"The righteous perish, and no one ponders it in his heart; devout men are taken away, and no one understands that the righteous are taken away to be spared from evil." (Isa. 57:1)

Praying
Together

Prayer for a Pastor's Child Who Has Strayed from the Lord

Heavenly Father, our hearts reach out for the child of our pastor. She once seemed so in love with you— so innocent, so devoted. Now her heart seems cold and distant. She has done things that bring shame to her father and mother. How we hurt for this family, Lord. It grieves our hearts to see this once happy family torn apart by sin.

Bring comfort to our pastor and his wife and conviction that you are in ultimate control. Hold the enemy at bay when he seeks to accuse and lay guilt on these parents. Give them grace for today, Lord, and hope for tomorrow.

Work on the heart of this child, God. Show her that she may run, but she cannot hide from you. Show her that love is the only real answer to life's questions. Show her that your love and the love of her parents are the way to joy and peace. Tug at the strings of her heart with cords of love. Cause the pleasures of the moment to become putrid. Allow her no joy in sin, Lord. Instead, remind her of her first love. Remind her of what waits for her in heaven and what waits for her in the arms of her parents. Through Christ who cares so very much, amen.

"Simon, Simon, Satan has asked to sift you as wheat. But I have prayed for you, Simon, that your faith may not fail. And when you have turned back, strengthen your brothers." (Luke 22:31)

Prayer for an Immoral Pastor

*L*ord, we see so much sin around us in the world; we never imagined it could invade our church. We grieve at the sin our pastor has committed. We feel angry and betrayed and hurt. We look back on the previous months and wonder how much his sin affected his ministering and how much it infected our body.

Then we look at ourselves, Lord, and realize we are not to judge, for we ourselves have fallen in many ways. We are no better or any worse than this man. Yet we know you don't want sin to remain or to rule.

Father, forgive his sins and cleanse our pastor of all that is not of you. He needs extra help, Lord, because he is on the front line of the battle—a prime target for Satan. Bring others around him that can bring our pastor healing and accountability.

Keep us from the effects of his sin, Lord, and let his experience be a frightening example of why we should flee immorality. Make us stronger through his weakness—not just as your servants, but as your body. Do not let Satan steal, kill, and destroy this man or this church. Take all the enemy means for evil and change it into good. In the name of Christ, amen.

"If we claim to be without sin, we deceive ourselves and the truth is not in us. If we confess our sins, he is faithful and just and will forgive us our sins and purify us from all unrighteousness." (1 John 1:8–9)

Refresh My Pastor Who Suffers from Burnout

*D*ear Father, we've watched for some time now as our pastor spends more and more time dealing with problems and has less and less time to spend focusing on you. He's tired, Lord, and has lost the spark and love for you that used to shine out every time he spoke.

O Lord, please help our pastor. Bring others around him to help shoulder the burden as Aaron and Hur did for Moses in the desert. Show him the things you have deemed most important for him to do. Give him a fresh sense of your presence in his life, Lord. Wash his soul with your Word in a way that touches and cleanses his heart. Give him new truths—not necessarily to share with others, but to treasure in his own heart—special and precious promises and blessings from you to him.

Bless his family too, Lord, and his marriage. Grant him priorities that allow for time away with his wife and time to interact with his kids for no special reason.

Finally, Lord, give him a new vision for where you are taking our church. Return a zeal and purpose to his ministry. Give him new ways to bring glory to you and new ways to bring people into your kingdom. Draw him close to you in worship and prayer, then burst forth grace from his life and the life of this church body, amen.

"After he had dismissed them, he went up into the hills by himself to pray." (Matt. 14:23)

Prayer Against Division in the Church

Our hearts break, O God, as we see the pain all around us. People who have loved and served each other now hurt and wound each other. We are a family, but how could brothers and sisters treat each other so badly? They all argue that they are right and others wrong, and in every instance they use your name to make their case! They strive to get their own way and satisfy their own selfish ambition, rather than submitting to the body of Christ and your Word. They have put on blinders, Lord. Their pride is hurt, and so they lash out, blaming others and defending themselves.

We are concerned for the young believers as well, Lord. What must it be like for them to look around and see the very people they have admired—their role models—striking out with words and actions designed to hurt and divide and separate?

God, drive us to prayer. Bring humility and love once again to our fellowship. Make the proud bow before you. Make the selfish see what they are really like as they stand before you, holy God. Let their hearts ache and their eyes tear when they think about the pain and disillusionment they are causing. Refocus our eyes on you and you alone as we lay our lives down before you as living sacrifices. Give us new priorities and a new calling. Help us all to see the vision you have for this church body. Through Christ we pray, amen.

"Finally, all of you, live in harmony with one another; be sympathetic, love as brothers, be compassionate and humble." (1 Peter 3:8)

Prayer for the Church
to Meet Needs

*G*reat Shepherd of the sheep, I cry to you for the needs of your church. How desperately your body of believers needs your help today. Guide those who oversee the church. Set spiritually-appointed, spiritually-anointed leadership in each pulpit. Shepherd those leaders in your ways and your will even as they lead your people. Cause us, as staff and congregants, to grow up together into wisdom and Christian maturity.

Give the pastors and elders your vision for their communities. Give unity. Fill these men and women with your mind and will and the courage to obey with no regard to the personal cost. Help leaders die to individual reputation and risk their faith when you say, "Go." Give courage to set God-ordered goals and priorities. Grant the faith to complete them. Help them release authority to godly lay leadership within the church. Then use leaders and laity to minister to each needy one that seeks help. Help us lead our friends and neighbors through the doors of our churches and into the fullness of your love and truth.

Let every need be met, Lord, so others find wholeness in you. Let no one slip through the cracks and go away hurting or hungry for answers. Empower your church with faith that we might be wonder workers, Father. Pour broken people through our doors; make them the recipients of the wondrous miracles only you can perform. The battle is yours, Lord. Help your church be strong and courageous, careful to obey, that we may bring souls to you. In the name of Jesus, amen.

"May the Lord make your love increase and overflow for each other and for everyone else, just as ours does for you. (1 Thess. 3:12–13)

A Prayer of Gratitude and Protection for Our Police Officers and Fire Fighters

*F*ather God, we thank you for the brave men and women who risk their lives daily to keep the people of our nation safe. No greater nobility exists than the willingness to lay down one's life for another. Our respect for these men and women deepens daily, and we pray for you to bless them in every way.

Dispense mighty angels to wrap them in protective wings as they engage in dangerous tasks. Send your Holy Spirit to give them wisdom and to keep them from taking unnecessary risks. Encourage decision makers to provide state-of-the-art equipment to make their jobs safer and more effective. Make the people of the nation continue to hold these police officers and fire fighters in high esteem. Keep public opinion on their side against the forces of evil. Call lawmakers to enforce the laws and punish perpetrators of all crimes, so the evil forces against these brave men and women won't seem so overwhelming.

We love them, Lord, and we want them to feel the depths of your fervent love. That's why we ask you to give them the gift of friendship with you. Call them irresistibly into your arms. Enter their hearts and be their source of constant peace. Let them feel fulfilled in you. We pray this in the name of Jesus, amen.

"If you make the Most High your dwelling . . . He will command his angels concerning you to guard you in all your ways . . . 'Because he loves me,' says the LORD, *'I will rescue him; I will protect him, for he acknowledges my name.'"* (Ps. 91:9, 11, 14)

Prayer for the Media

*H*eavenly Father, we thank you for the media—entertainers, producers, newscasters, writers, radio personalities, and publishers—all those who speak to the country on an ongoing basis. Their talents and intellect impress us. We are grateful for their unflagging efforts to entertain us and enlighten us concerning events around the world.

But they don't always represent you fairly, God. The news media rarely mentions you; radio and television spew vulgar language; movies openly portray Christians in a bad light. That is wrong, and we cry out against it! Remove the acceptance and glorification of evil from television, motion pictures, and the written word.

Reveal your love to the unbelieving representatives of the media and turn their hearts toward you. Set more of your true followers in positions of power and influence. Infuse reporters, actors, writers, and directors with a mindset that glorifies your standards. Lead them to present you fairly and honestly. Transmit your values across the airwaves; undergird everything spoken or written with your perfect love. Let the media delight to share your principles with the world. Then pour out blessings on them. We ask this in Jesus' name, amen.

"The heart of the righteous weight its answers, but the mouth of the wicked gushes evil." (Prov. 15:28)

Prayer for
College-Bound Students

*F*ather, our young people—our idealists, our risk-takers, our explorers, and our independence-seekers—are heading off to colleges and universities all over the world. We have spent years loving, guiding, and teaching them in your Word, but now they are off on their own.

Thank you for the opportunities this year will offer: seeing new places, collecting new experiences, exploring new ideas, meeting new people, and making new friends. May they meet these challenges confidently and enthusiastically. Help them develop the self-discipline and study skills necessary to complete their courses.

Guard them physically from accidental harm, whether they're on campus or driving around with friends or playing sports. Protect them from those who would hurt them intentionally. Give them discernment in classes and casual discussions. Don't allow ungodly professors to undermine their faith. Guide them to develop a personal worldview based on the Bible.

Help them choose friends who will encourage and not discourage them in their walk with you. Protect them from the evil one, who would destroy their testimony and their lives through alcohol and drugs, accumulation of debt, sexual promiscuity, and other temptations. When they're depressed, lonely, homesick, brokenhearted, stressed, or grappling with major issues, please provide a wise Christian friend or mentor for them.

Stretch them spiritually. Develop within them a deep love for you, your Word, and the family of God. Open up opportunities for them to share their faith and serve others.

Guide them as they define who they are and how to make important decisions about their careers or future spouses. And Lord? Every so often, let life be a blast! In the name of the One who brings joy to life, amen.

"How can a young man keep his way pure? By living according to your word." (Ps. 119:9)

Prayer for American Students Abroad

Wonderful Father, what a comfort to know that you are sovereign. We praise you that all things are under your control—families, governments, even the daily circumstances of our lives. Thank you that you care about the smallest detail that concerns your children. We're so grateful, Lord, that you've taught us to pray. Thank you for leaning over the balconies of heaven, even now, and listening as we pray for our American students abroad.

Give safety as they travel, Lord. At every point of need surround them with helpful people who can answer their questions. Protect them, God. Help them be aware of their surroundings and make wise choices. Settle them into new homes with a minimum of loneliness and stress. Provide instant friends—young and old—who will share their lives and love them as we do. Provide mentors to encourage and guide them as they study and mature.

Thank you, Father, that you will be with them while they are away. Your promise is that you will never leave us or forsake us, and we claim that word for these students. Keep them growing spiritually. Even in the strangeness of foreign places, keep them centered each day in the security of your familiar presence. Remind them to read their Bibles and pray. Fulfill your plans for them, and bring them home again, safe and sound, amen.

"The LORD bless you and keep you; the LORD make his face shine upon you and be gracious to you; the LORD turn his face toward you and give you peace." (Num. 6:24–26)

Prayer for Foreign Students in the United States

*F*ather, thank you for the opportunity American families have to host young people from other countries. Place it on the hearts of Christian families to open their homes to these foreign students.

These young people are far from home, away from all that is familiar, and away from family and friends. Help them adjust to differing social customs, conversing in a language foreign to them, a new currency, different transportation systems, attending unfamiliar schools, and other students' attitudes.

They will be exposed to all aspects of our culture and society, the good and the bad. They will absorb ideas that will affect the rest of their lives. Many of them fear the violence in America. Keep them safe from harm and from unknowingly placing themselves in dangerous situations. Direct them to loving Christians who will introduce them to the Savior.

Give us all a vision for reaching people from other cultures right here at home. In Jesus' name, amen.

"Do not forget to entertain strangers, for by so doing some people have entertained angels without knowing it." (Heb. 13:2)

A Prayer for Church Attendees Who Don't Know God

O Lord, our hearts are burdened for people who attend church but may not actually know you. We don't know who they are, Lord, but you do, because you see into their hearts. They're just filling a time slot, putting a checkmark on a list, fooling themselves that they please you by showing up to sit in a pew. They may hear the pastor's words, but their ears are shut to your whispers. Some of them leave the service and live immoral lives during the week. Others simply choose not to develop a friendship with you.

We're afraid for them, Lord. You said many would arrive in heaven thinking they belong to you when they don't. You said you would command them to leave your presence! Don't let that prophecy be fulfilled in our church, Lord.

Grab the attitudes and actions of lukewarm Christians, Lord! Knock them to their knees in repentance. Warm hearts of stone until they burn with longing for you. I pray by the power of your Holy Spirit that church attendees who don't have a relationship with you would cry out from the depths of their souls for more of you. Show them what it means to desperately love you, the God of the universe. Enter into an intimate love relationship with them. Let them return your passionate love. In Jesus' name, amen.

"These people come near to me with their mouth and honor me with their lips, but their hearts are far from me. Their worship is made up only of rules taught by men." (Is. 29:13)

"Then I will tell them plainly, 'I never knew you. Away from me you evildoers.'" (Matt. 7:23)

God, Save Gang Members

*L*oving heavenly Father, you created a perfect world for us. You wanted us to feel fulfilled, so you set us in families with a mother and a father who would love us and teach us your ways. But the world isn't perfect anymore; broken families rarely meet needs. Lonely children wander the streets, searching for love. And many make wrong choices—evil choices.

Forgive them, Lord. Forgive them for the violence they inflict on rival gang members and innocent bystanders. Forgive their aberrant sexual behavior. Forgive insensitive hearts that refuse to understand or care when they cause pain. Forgive them for disrespecting their own bodies with drugs and alcohol. Forgive them when they fail to understand your love, because you do love them . . . no matter how wicked they've been.

Lord, call them to repentance. Rip the veil of darkness from their minds and let them see the ugliness of their own sin. Let it disgust them. Make them long for righteousness. You can do this no matter how hard they seem; no matter how bad they are.

When they turn their hearts to you, direct them seek out your family in churches. Open the eyes of your established family so they are able to look past gang apparel and recognize a new baby in Christ. Let family love overflow to these former gang members as you settle them into the family of God. We praise you for your loving kindness and mercy, which comes through Christ, amen.

"God sets the lonely in families, he leads forth the prisoners with singing; but the rebellious live in a sun-scorched land." (Ps. 68:6)

Grant Guidance When a Boss Is Difficult

*G*od of hope, we've come today for a new supply of patience and grace. Our boss is absolutely impossible to please. No matter what we do, he finds fault. We're all good employees, Lord, organized and capable—turning in our work on time. You know how often we help each other so everything stays on schedule. Yet he constantly complains. None of us can remember one time he has ever said thank you or affirmed us. All he does is growl and scowl. It's so discouraging. Some take sick time just to get away from him for a day. This situation is affecting the whole office. Depression hangs like a cloud over our heads.

Lord, we don't want to be bitter and angry. We want to please you with a right attitude, no matter what happens at work. But God, we're so filled with resentment. Please change our boss. Give us, as employees, your grace or your answer. One of your character traits is justice, so we appeal to your justice and mercy, Lord. Your Word says we're to cast our anxiety upon you, so we're rolling this problem onto your shoulders, Father. We're asking you to deal with him and his attitudes. You made him, Lord, so we know you can speak to his heart. Thank you. Help us all get up and go to work again tomorrow in your strength, amen.

"May our Lord Jesus Christ himself and God our Father . . . encourage your hearts and strengthen you in every good word and deed." (2 Thess. 2:16–17)

Help Us Resolve
Work Conflicts

*L*ord, we need your help again. Thank you for encouraging us to come to you with our needs and problems. The Bible says we should ask and seek and knock until the answers come, so here we are, seeking your wisdom for this difficult woman at work. Lord, we've done everything humanly possible to be her friends, yet she makes us all the brunt of her office jokes. She ignores job responsibilities. Instead of cooperating on projects, she seems determined to create dissension. We're so tired of it all, Lord. Show us, as people who must work together, what to do. Help us know how to respond.

Defend our reputations when we're slandered before others. Vindicate us as you've promised to do. Teach us whether to confront her or ignore the problem.

Is this a spiritual battle? Is the enemy deliberately creating tension between us so that we won't love her and speak your truth? Show us the answers, Lord, one day at a time. Give everyone grace and faith for today. Help us listen for your counsel. Teach us all how to handle this problem. We pray through the One who loves and understands, amen.

"In all these things we are more than conquerors through him who loved us." (Rom. 8:37)

Give Us Courage to Stand Against Wrong Principles

*L*ord, you have taught your people that you are holy and require holiness of each Christian. As followers of you, we love your ways. Your Word has brought us into wholeness. Yet so many in the business world—where we work every day—feel our views are legalistic, intolerant, and restrictive of personal freedom. They aren't willing to accept your Word as the only standard. They surround us, Lord, often wanting to argue against the absolutes of the Bible. Help us speak the truth in love to them.

Empower us to share your truth unashamedly in our offices and businesses. Keep us from being overbearing or argumentative. Give each of us love for those who don't agree with our position. Open their hearts to seek you, Lord. Overwhelm their defenses with the logic of truth. Help us all to be wise as serpents, but harmless as doves as we talk with these unbelievers. Help us be undaunted when rebuked or ridiculed for our stand. Cause our lives to bear such fabulous fruit that everyone will see that you bless those who follow your Word. Make them hungry for you, Lord, when they watch the lives of Christians. Bridge us, as we work each day, to those who are truth seekers—those who will yet come to love you. Change their mindsets through our words and actions. Help us love them into your kingdom. Thank you, Lord, amen.

"If you do not stand firm in your faith, you will not stand at all." (Isa. 7:9)

Fulfill Your Purpose for Christian Business

Sovereign Lord, we bring Christian businesses to you in prayer. We are burdened for businesses you have planted across the world and in the United States. You had a specific purpose when you formed each corporation, Lord. You predetermined in your will and mind what direction each company was to go; what services and products they should provide. You selected leadership and employees for each group, anticipating their success.

But Lord, many presidents and CEOs of the Christian firms you birthed have never gotten on their knees and sought you for godly principles by which to run their businesses. Instead, they limp along, mired in a secular mindset, wondering why they can't make budget; why their company doesn't grow. They have no corporate vision. They don't know your true purpose for their firm, and therefore they cannot implement your plan. You said that without your vision we perish. Surely that is true of corporations also.

Only wise God, burden these leaders to seek your mind so they will have success. Help them get on their faces before you and stay there until you have given them your vision statement for their company. Help them treat their employees honestly, paying wages and benefits that honor those who serve them. Cause them to be fair with customers; honorable in all things. Don't let corporate leadership compromise truth, Lord. Help each Christian company bring glory to you as they serve the business community. Thank you, Father, amen.

"Be careful to obey all the law my servant Moses gave you; do not turn from it to the right or to the left, that you may be successful wherever you go." (Josh. 1:7)

Grant Stability for the Stock Market

God of the nations, your Word says that the love of money is a root of all kinds of evil; greed can cause people to wander from the faith. We know the stock market has fed that greed many times, Lord, and we stand against the love of money. We pray that investors will not make financial gain their god.

But the fact is, Lord, today's world economy depends on a stable stock market, and so we petition you for steady, reliable growth on Wall Street. We don't ask for easy wealth for investors; we simply request a solid economy that will provide jobs and meet needs.

We know you want to bless us, Lord. Give us right hearts and attitudes so you can. In Jesus' name we pray, amen.

"For the love of money is a root of all kinds of evil. Some people, eager for money, have wandered from the faith and pierced themselves with many griefs." (1 Tim. 6:19)

"Give me neither poverty nor riches, but give me only my daily bread. Otherwise, I may have too much and disown you and say, 'Who is the LORD?' Or I may become poor and steal, and so dishonor the name of my God." (Prov. 30:8–9)

Prayer for an Uncertain Future

*T*hank you, dear God, for your promise to never leave us or forsake us. Your promise helps to still our fears as we face an uncertain future. Your promise assures us we won't walk through any valley alone, for you are a Good Shepherd who will stay by us as you guide us through this dark valley.

Amid all the uncertainty that surrounds us, we want our eyes to remain focused on you and not on our worries or fears. We want to hold on to your promise with all our might. When our sights are fixed on you, fear-filled thoughts and circumstances will no longer be able to overwhelm or paralyze us. You are our helper. We will not be afraid with you at our side.

We trust you as we confidently walk forward into this day. You will help us face the uncertainty of our future. Thank you for being a reliable helper in time of need. Thank you for all you have done and will continue to do for us. In Jesus' name, amen.

"God has said, 'Never will I leave you; never will I forsake you.' So we say with confidence, 'The Lord is my helper; I will not be afraid. What can man do to me?'" (Heb. 13:5–6)

A Plea to Stand Firm Amidst Frightening Changes

O God our Savior, we thank you for the blessings you have poured down on our nation over the years. We have come to expect prosperity. We take our jobs and luxurious homes for granted. We can't imagine anything less than supermarkets piled high with fresh meat and produce.

But things have begun to change, holy Father. Earthquakes rock the globe. Disease obliterates whole herds of animals. Record droughts and flooding threaten crops and homes. Pictures of starving children flicker across our television screens. The AIDS virus threatens to wipe half the people from the continent of Africa. Terrorists rip away our security.

Lord, we wonder, why? Did you send the disaster to correct us and turn us back to yourself? Or have you simply allowed those terrible things?

The truth is, God, we don't know the answer. We only know that we welcome your righteousness. We beg for your protection while the world seems to fall apart around us. In the midst of the disasters we submit to you, we ask you to teach and perfect us through them. We plead for your quick return. And while we wait on you, Lord, we will praise you. We will be joyful in you.

"Though the fig tree does not bud and there are no grapes on the vines, though the olive crop fails and the fields produce no food, though there are no sheep in the pen and no cattle in the stalls, yet I will rejoice in the LORD, I will be joyful in God my Savior." (Hab. 3:17–18)

Praise for God's Faithfulness in Tough Times

O Lord God, we praise you for your mercy and love—love as high as the heavens and as deep as the oceans. We give thanks that your faithfulness sustains us, even though present circumstances threaten to overwhelm us. We know you are greater than every problem and more powerful than every evil that may come against us.

Keep our eyes fixed on you, O Lord. Keep us mindful of your promises and your tender care. Pour out your glory over all the earth during these hard times. Touch every heart with the comfort of your presence and the assurance of your care. Your eyes are on the sparrow and we know you watch us also.

Help us share your goodness and mercy with others during these times. Give us opportunities to encourage each other. Help us to continue to trust you and to thank you for all you have done and all you will do.

O Lord, we praise you. We exalt you above all the troubles and cares of this day. We sing of your goodness and faithfulness. Help us rise up in faith and courage, for you alone are our faithful Father and friend. We worship you through Jesus Christ, our Lord, amen.

"I will praise you, O LORD, among the nations; I will sing of you among the peoples. For great is your love, reaching to the heavens; your faithfulness reaches to the skies. Be exalted, O God, above the heavens; let your glory be over all the earth." (Ps. 57:9–11)

Prayer for Our President

*D*ear Lord, thank you for the privilege of praying for our president. You have put him in authority over us. Help us to be good citizens by lifting him up in prayer regularly. We are grateful, Father, that he has accepted Jesus as his personal Savior. Please draw him even to closer to you so he can guide our nation according to your principles.

Help us to remember that in spite of all the trappings of his office, he is merely a man. Give him the humility to realize this and, as Solomon did, to turn to you for wisdom to lead our nation. Remind him that his power comes from you, and that he is ultimately accountable to you for his actions.

Give him the physical, psychological, and spiritual stamina needed to carry out his presidential duties. Place alongside him wise and moral advisors who will uphold your principles. Strengthen him when he is weak; support him when he is attacked.

Make him not only a leader of our nation, but help him to be the leader of his family as well. Strengthen his relationships with his wife and children. Help him learn to put aside the duties of his office for short periods of time to nourish and be nourished by them.

As president, he is already a model for many people, young and old. Make him a man of stature, at home and abroad, upholding the principles of our nation. And sometimes, let him laugh, amen

"So give your servant a discerning heart to govern your people and to distinguish between right and wrong. For who is able to govern this great people of yours?" (1 Kings 3:9)

Prayer for Supreme Court Justices

O God, you are just and loving. In your Word you have spelled out the way we are to relate to others. Our laws are based on these commandments. Thank you for them; we know that when we follow these laws, they preserve order in our country.

We pray right now for the justices at each level of our judicial system, especially our Supreme Court justices. We pray for their salvation, for moral integrity, for clear consciences informed by your Word, for courage to make difficult decisions, and for wisdom in deciding complicated cases.

Give these men and women clarity of thought and purity of heart. Strengthen their character so corrupt participants, eloquent lawyers, a critical media, a passionate populace, or even their own career aspirations will not sway them. Guide their minds and wills so they are willing to submit their decisions to the principles of our nation's founding documents and your Word.

And Lord, it must be lonely at times to carry the responsibility for making decisions that affect people's lives so deeply. For those who turn to you for wisdom, give them the comfort and assurance of your presence, and from time to time may they hear your words, "Well done, good and faithful servant." Thank you, Lord, amen.

"When justice is done, it brings joy to the righteous but terror to evildoers." (Prov. 21:15)

Prayer for Our Cabinet Members

*D*ear God, there are so many civil servants who are invisible to us, or at least not a part of our daily consciousness. Right now we think of the members of the president's cabinet—people who influence the president and make important decisions in the departments they oversee.

We ask that the president would choose men and women of personal integrity and competence in the area of their expertise. And our desire is that each person in the cabinet would come to know Jesus Christ as Savior.

We pray for accuracy in the information gathered and reported, wisdom to sort out complex issues, and a willingness to work as team and put the good of the country above personal career goals.

Give them a good grasp of the issues they face. May the advice they offer the president when he creates domestic and foreign policies be sound. Give them insight into the consequences of their decisions and creative solutions to difficult problems. Help them realize the insufficiency of human knowledge, and give them the humility to turn to you for wisdom.

Thank you for their willingness to serve our country. Honor their efforts with success, we pray. In Jesus' name, amen.

"For he is God's servant to do you good." (Rom. 13:4)

Prayer for Our Senators and Representatives

*H*eavenly Father, thank you that ordinary people like us have a voice in our national government. Thank you for our senators and representatives who choose a life of public service. Give us men and women who believe in your Son, who will truly serve the country, and who will refuse to play the game of power politics. May they be people of personal integrity who make decisions within a moral framework based on your Word and the founding documents of this country.

Help them balance their responsibilities to represent the people of their states with the needs of the country as a whole. Give them wisdom when lobbyists with special interests press them. And may they put principles and the people of this country above party loyalty and politics.

Guide them in the hiring of trustworthy staffers who will give them honest reports. Grant them knowledge and understanding to judge complex issues. Help them not to play fast and loose with the laws they make, the people they represent, or the finances they control. Keep them faithful to their wives and families, and may their families support them in their service to our country.

Give those who are Christians an extra measure of wisdom, the courage to openly share their faith, the love to reach out to others, and the strength to withstand added pressure. In Jesus' name, amen.

"This is also why you pay taxes, for the authorities are God's servants, who give their full time to governing." (Rom. 13:6)

Prayer for Our Governor

*F*ather, thank you for allowing us to live under a government where we can choose our leaders and thank you for allowing us to make our home in this beautiful state that we love so dearly.

We pray for our governor, who is responsible for the welfare of all of us in this state. Bring him to a saving knowledge of your Son. Help him maintain integrity in both his personal and public life. Help him keep his moral compass in a world of financial demands, competing interests, deals and compromises, and conflicting political loyalties. Don't let the trappings of power blind him to his responsibility.

In the inevitable juggling of time and priorities, show him the true value of his wife and family. Help him make the commitments necessary to strengthen these relationships. In Jesus' name, amen.

"Everyone must submit himself to the governing authorities, for there is no authority except that which God has established. The authorities that exist have been established by God." (Rom. 13:1)

Prayer for Local and State Government Officials

*F*ather, our local government leaders influence our daily lives with their decisions. Help us become informed voters; aware of the issues and those who represent us. Grant each one the opportunity to choose Jesus Christ as his or her Savior from a life ruled by sin.

These men and women are learning the art of statecraft. May they bring to their offices high moral standards. Help them learn to compromise where appropriate, but also give them the courage to stand firm in moral matters. Give them wisdom in their dealings with people and issues as they balance conflicting wants, needs, and expectations.

Help them to carry out their duties conscientiously, by giving their best in their present jobs, and not viewing them merely as stepping stones to higher offices.

Lord, remind us of our responsibility to be involved and to pray before we criticize. May we truly be part of the solution, and not part of the problem. In Jesus' name, amen.

"I urge, then, first of all, that requests, prayers, intercession and thanksgiving be made for everyone—for kings and all those in authority, that we may live peaceful and quiet lives in all godliness and holiness." (1 Tim. 2:1–2)

Prayer for "We the People"

*F*ather God, we are so grateful to live in a country founded by men who acknowledged you as the source of our rights and our freedoms, men who called on you for wisdom as they formed our national laws and ideals. We understand that "we the people" are the government. The men and women who represent us at every level of government are drawn from our neighborhoods, elected by our choices.

Father, turn the hearts of Americans to you and your Word. Forgive us for abandoning the basic moral tenets that honor you and protect us and those around us. Build into our lives the character traits we need to maintain our free society: dependence on you, personal integrity, commitment to justice, love and respect for our fellow citizens, generosity to the needy, and courage to stand against evil.

Thank you for those who govern us. They are imperfect, making decisions that sometimes hearten us and sometimes dismay us, but you have said these men and women are acting as your servants to protect us from evildoers and allow us to live orderly, quiet lives. Our leaders have a great number of responsibilities and just as many temptations. Give them the wisdom to see truth and the courage to make moral decisions. Give us the strength to support them where appropriate and hold them accountable when necessary. And O God, turn our hearts, and the hearts of our leaders back to you. In Jesus' name, amen.

"If my people, who are called by my name, will humble themselves and pray and seek my face and turn from their wicked ways, then will I hear from heaven and will forgive their sin and will heal their land." (2 Chron. 7:14)

O Lord, Forgive Our Sons and Daughters for Their Abortions

ather God, our hearts are breaking. Our sons and our darling daughters, in times of depression and fear, have aborted their own babies. It is done. There is nothing we can do to prevent this horror. Oh, God, we cannot stop weeping for these men and women, for the babies, and for your broken heart. Lord, forgive this hideous sin and everyone involved—parents who pressured them, teachers who referred them to clinics, doctors who killed the babies, and the society who devalues life. Forgive us for not being there in their moments of desperation.

O God, help them. Many of them love you. They must be horrified at what they found themselves capable of doing. Help them cry out to you in their agony and depression. Help them repent so you can forgive; so they can forgive themselves. Wrap them in your loving arms. Show them that there is nothing you can't cover in love. Convince them, Lord, that nothing can separate them from your love. Lord, don't let them block this from their minds and spirits. Don't let them justify what they have done; for without repentance they cannot know forgiveness. Help them face themselves, Father, and accept your mercy. Create clean hearts in our sons and daughters, Lord. Somehow, give grace and use this for good. Mend broken hearts with your unfailing love, merciful God. Amen.

"Have mercy on me, O God, according to your unfailing love; according to your great compassion blot out my transgressions. . . . Restore to me the joy of your salvation and grant me a willing spirit, to sustain me." (Ps. 51:1,12)

Forgive Our Failure to Protect Our Children

O gracious and holy Father, we bow before you in shame. You blessed us with children—the most precious treasure you can give—and we have failed to protect them.

Forgive us for labeling every sin a disorder; for making excuses for perpetrators who inflict vile and immoral behavior on our innocents. Forgive us when we don't cry out against the violence in the media that desensitizes our youth. Forgive us for condoning pornography under freedom of speech, while denying prayer as a violation of the separation between church and state. Forgive us for including sexual impurity under the titles of diversity and political correctness. Forgive us for choosing our own selfish satisfaction above the happiness of our children and allowing guilt-free divorce to smash their security. Forgive us when glitzy sitcoms persuade young girls that unmarried intimacy is acceptable and glamorous. Forgive us when society's loose moral standards deprive babies of fathers. Forgive us for stripping teachers of the power to hold children accountable in the classroom. Forgive us for providing realistic video games that portray murder and train youths to kill. Forgive us when these false foundations beneath us crumble and children kill children in the war zones we call schools.

Forgive us when veiled eyes cannot perceive that our habit of cherishing sin erodes our nation. Father, forgive us, through Christ, amen.

"Jesus said, 'Father, forgive them, for they do not know what they are doing.'" (Luke 23:34)

Help the Family of This Child Molester

O Lord, our hearts go out the family of this child molester. The shock and horror of his deeds have shaken them to the depths of their being. They didn't know, Lord, yet they feel so guilty. Shame covers them like a heavy fog, yet it won't hide them. They feel as though everyone knows and blames them. Show them that isn't true. You know they are innocent of this evil, Lord. The molester made the choices; not them. Assure them it isn't their fault. They didn't see the sin he hid so well. Release them from this undeserved shame.

God, carry them through the sorrow and grief they will have to endure because of his actions. Give them strength to ask you for your help. Show them how to love him while totally rejecting his sin and refusing to make excuses for him. Help them understand that continuing to love the molester is not shameful; you love us even though you hate our sin. Help them stand firm through this, Lord, knowing their help comes from you. We praise you for your righteousness. Through the Righteous One we pray, amen.

"Fathers shall not be put to death for their children, nor children put to death for their fathers; each is to die for his own sin." (Deut. 24:16)

A Cry Against Violence in Our Nation and World

O God who judges all the earth, you see each act of violence that strikes the people of our nation and the world. Nothing is hidden from you. How your heart must ache when you see Christians tortured and killed simply for speaking your name! How your anger must burn against evil governments who foster terrorists and steal food from the mouths of their poor!

Violence spills from movie screens and televisions—seeping out into the street where rapes and drive-by shootings are so numerous they no longer make the news. Even our children feast on violent video games, then snatch up guns and murder their schoolmates. Lord, how grieved you must feel!

God, could Noah's world have been more violent than ours? I don't see how. And you destroyed them, Lord. You wiped them off the face of the earth. Do we deserve to be treated differently?

Have mercy on us, Lord! Save us! Forgive us! Change us! Turn our nation and our world to righteousness so that peace and security will reign. Send a revival of your Spirit to sweep away the violence and replace our evil thoughts with thoughts of you. Help us to acknowledge you as our God. We know you can do this, Lord. We beg for your mercy in Jesus' name, amen.

"So God said to Noah, 'I have decided to destroy all living creatures, for the earth is filled with violence because of them.'" (Gen. 6:13 NLT)

A Prayer Against the Plague of Divorce

*D*ear God, we're so thankful you are the author of marriage. It was your idea that a man and his wife would be united as one. You made the perfect plan, but you knew we would be far from perfect—which can make marriage challenging.

There are many couples in the church and the world who think divorce is the answer to marriage problems. Show them the truth—divorce causes heartache. It is a sin. It is painful. It does not just affect the couple involved, but all those around them, especially the children. Lord, we pray for your hand of restoration to overshadow our nation. Change hearts, priorities, work schedules, and lives. Bring healing and forgiveness to the institution of marriage.

We pray for our pastors and church leaders to take a new stand—a stronger stand—for marriage. Give them boldness to speak out and contradict the lies we have believed regarding divorce.

Turn the hearts of those with healthy, godly marriages toward couples who are struggling. Give them the desire, the time, and the skills to come alongside and mentor those people. Start with the church, Lord. Let the world see what a beautiful gift marriage can be when Jesus Christ is at the center.

Teach us to take our eyes off ourselves and place them first on you and then on our spouses. We look to your Word as the standard, and we remember that you have bound us together in holy matrimony. Teach us to be holy. In the name of the Holy One, we pray, amen.

"Wives, submit to your husbands, as is fitting in the Lord. Husbands, love your wives and do not be harsh with them." (Col. 3:18–19)

We Confess Our Sins

O gracious and holy God, we are overwhelmed with sorrow because of our sins. We confess them to you, but we know confession is not enough. Repentance must reach deep into our hearts and dig out the rebellion that makes us forget you. It can't be a superficial repentance brought on because we have suffered and don't want to hurt anymore. We must repent because every sin is against *you*, the only holy God!

After David's affair with Bathsheba, he said he had sinned against you only, God. Even though he murdered Uriah and others died in the process. Even though he sinned against Bathsheba, his own family, and the entire country of Israel, he declared that he had sinned against *you* only.

O God, we too have sinned against you, the sinless, perfect Creator of the universe, who loves us with an everlasting love! Our sins have caused you pain and grief. Forgive us, Lord. Make us new! Grant us the determination and strength to turn from our wicked ways. Help us walk worthy of your love. Thank you, Lord. We pray in the name of the Sinless One, amen.

"*Against you, you only, have I sinned and done what is evil in your sight.*" (Ps. 51:4)

Crying Out for National Revival

*L*ord, national crisis strips away our self-sufficiency and our superficial concerns, and opens our eyes to our desperate need for you. Our founding fathers acknowledged you as the source of our freedoms, God. We remember their warning that our nation would last only as long as we lived according to your Ten Commandments. We no longer do that, Lord. Many in our country have tried to outlaw and destroy your basic moral principles. Your enemy has filled our bellies with the refuge of self-indulgence and the rot of sexual deviancy and violence. We despise that, Lord. We fall on our faces before you. Have mercy on us! Drench us with your Holy Spirit. Pour it out in rushing torrents that flush us clean! Irresistibly draw us back to you.

We repent of our many and vile sins. Change us! Purify us in your fire. Purge our apathy. Rip the scales from our eyes. Banish dullness from our ears. Awaken in us a hunger and a burning desire and for the high and holy! Beckon us to humble ourselves and fervently call out to you. Cause us to desire you more than your gifts. We invite you back into our hearts, back into our churches, and back into our schools. We choose obedience to your commands. We submit to you as King of our lives and King of our nation. Come, Lord Jesus, come. We praise you for your goodness and mercy! Amen.

"Blessed is the nation whose God is the Lord.*"* (Ps. 33:12)

Prayer for People Dragged into Court

*D*ear heavenly Father, adversaries drag innocent people into court, confusing them and filling them with vague uneasiness, guilt, and fear. They worry they may lose the case, and the authorities could take everything they own. They wonder how they will pay attorneys.

Remove fears about finances, Lord. Show them you will provide for them. Show them they need feel no guilt, God. Help them fight resentment and anger because they think they have been treated unfairly. Help them turn it over to you, God, forgiving anyone who has wronged them.

Give them wise, fair judges, Lord, and hold all witnesses to strict honesty. Grant them courage to speak truthfully if they are called to testify. When they open their mouths, let your words come out just as you promised. Supply faith for them to trust you completely. Fill them with confidence that no matter what happens, they are in your hands and you always work everything out for good. Then grant them justice. We ask this in Jesus' name, amen.

"Whenever you are arrested and brought to trial, do not worry beforehand about what to say. Just say whatever is given you at the time, for it is not you speaking, but the Holy Spirit." (Mark 13:11)

Prayer in the Aftermath of Natural Disasters

*H*eavenly Father, floods, hurricanes, and tornadoes leave your people trembling in fear. The very sky seems to be their enemy, gathering whirling winds and then hurling that power at homes, churches, and schools, pouring down huge quantities of water that collapse buildings and drag people into raging currents. Nothing feels safe to them anymore. The electricity is out; they have no shelter, and little food. They wait in lines for clean water; disease spreads through the community. And the water continues to rise. They wonder if you did this to them, God. Have you withdrawn your love from them?

They're exhausted. They work from dawn till dark filling sandbags to hold back the water, then cleaning, salvaging . . . crying. They're worried about everything, God: jobs, loved ones, where they will live. They've lost everything—except you.

Reach out to them, Lord. Assure them of your love. Show them you are there to rescue them. You haven't left them; you're working beside them, surrounding weary hands with your hands, lifting tired arms when shovels and brooms seem too heavy. You give strength. You give the ability to endure this trial. Help them to reach out and accept your help. Show them that nothing can separate them from your love. With you beside them they *will* make it through this victoriously, and you'll build godly character through suffering.

"And I am convinced that nothing can ever separate us from his love. Death can't, and life can't. The angels can't, and the demons can't. Our fears for today, or worries about tomorrow, and even the powers of hell can't keep God's love away." (Rom. 8:38 NLT)

Protect Us in the Midst
of Earthquakes

O God, the very earth you created shook us in its fury. Windows rattled and broke; buildings collapsed. We're terrified, God. If the earth itself seeks to destroy us, where can we find safety?

We barely recognize the land where our homes once stood. We search for shelter from the quaking, but there is no place to hide. No building feels safe; weakened foundations threaten to crumble with each new aftershock. What are we to do, Lord? Where can we turn?

We fear fire and disease. We work all day trying to locate the bare necessities we need just to survive. Do you see us, God? Do you care about us? Will we ever feel safe? Will you provide homes again?

Protect us, Lord. Provide for us. Let us feel your love. Give us faith in your mercies. Help us relinquish our fears to you. You will care for us, God. You do love us. We know you have not abandoned us. Though everything around us falls, and nothing but rubble remains, we determine to trust in you. You are our home. We will take refuge in you. Thank you, God!

"Lord, through all the generations you have been our home!" (Ps. 90:1 NLT)

"My soul finds rest in God alone; my salvation comes from him. He alone is my rock and my salvation; he is my fortress, I will never be shaken." (Ps. 62:1–2)

Help Us Not to Fear a Terrorist Attack

*T*hank you, dear God, for your love, your mercy, and your promises. Calm our minds and hearts today as rumors abound concerning terrorist plots, schemes, and activities. We feel overwhelmed with the terrorists' immense hatred directed toward our country and toward us as Americans and Christians.

O God, we need your help. Replace our fear with faith. Replace our dismay with hope. Help us focus our eyes and thoughts on you instead of on what a terrorist could do to harm our loved ones or us. We want to fix our thoughts on you and your goodness rather than on the evil of terrorism in our world this day. We want to set our sights on your promises rather than any fears of what "might" happen in the event of a terrorist attack.

You are our God, and we trust you will keep every one of your promises. Place your perfect peace within us as we focus our minds on you. Strengthen us and help us, no matter what happens. Don't let us be overcome with worry or despair. Let your love and mercy always triumph over evil, hatred, and injustice. Help us in times of trouble.

You are all we need this day. You will hold our lives, our families, and our country in your hand. Now help us rest in your strong right hand and lean on your Son, our Savior, Jesus, amen.

"So do not fear, for I am with you; do not be dismayed, for I am your God. I will strengthen you and help you; I will uphold you with my righteous right hand." (Is. 41:10)

A Prayer for Individual Terrorists

ompassionate, loving Father, terrorists are men deluded by your enemy, held firmly in Satan's grasp. We denounce their evil actions. Lord, these men gorge on murderous fantasies, dreaming up new cruelties every day, reveling in the pain they inflict, and thirsting for the deaths of innocent people.

Their leaders persuade them to adulate murder and suicide as holy acts. These men believe they are acting righteously, Lord. How tragic that they eagerly anticipate paradise and wake up in hell! Our hearts ache for them. We lift them up to you with holy hands, begging you to have mercy on their souls. Lift Satan's veil of filthy lies from their hearts, Father. Open their eyes to see and reject the savage perversion their leaders vomit over the airwaves. Reveal your holiness to them. Change them. Draw them to repentance.

If they will not turn and repent of their wickedness and forsake it, however, God, give them no peace. Destroy them before they kill more innocents and contaminate the hearts of their own people. We pray in Jesus' holy name, amen.

"But the wicked are like the tossing sea, which cannot rest, whose waves cast up mire and mud. 'There is no peace,' says my God, 'for the wicked.'" (Is. 57:20-21)

"But the people's minds were hardened, and even to this day . . . a veil covers their minds so they cannot understand the truth. And this veil can be removed only be believing in Christ." (2 Cor. 3:14 NLT)

O God, Defeat Terrorism

*L*ord, mighty in battle, we claim you as our God, our defender. You are holy; we are not. Yet, though our sins are many, our Pledge of Allegiance still affirms your lordship over us; we remain "one nation *under God.*" Those words give us boldness to request your help.

Our cause is just. We battle terrorism—a wicked force that exhausts fortunes and plots horror, then strikes simultaneously against unsuspecting people. It murders thousands of innocent victims in one swoop. We denounce the evil, Lord, and we beg for your power to defeat it. Terrorism lurks in holes and caves, waiting to pounce on our young men. We cry out against it, beseeching you for your protection. Terrorism spits in your face, Holy God, proclaiming a false god as the only god, usurping your throne. Let your name be glorified instead, Jehovah. Show yourself strong, take your rightful place, and prove that you are the only true God.

We go forth as your foot soldiers, willing to fight and die for freedom and justice. We are confident of success because we know it comes from you alone. Smash our fear. Demolish terrorism. Claim the victory, Lord. Shine forth as King of all kings, amen.

"Arise, O LORD, let not man triumph; let the nations be judged in your presence. Strike them with terror, O LORD; let the nations know they are but men." (Ps. 9:19–20)

A Grateful Family's Praise after a Terrorist Attack

O precious Father, how can we ever thank you enough for sparing the life of our loved one after that horrendous explosion? We still can't believe she made it out alive, Lord. We don't want to let her out of our sight. We just want to hold her and tell her how much we love her. Thank you, Lord, that you covered our loved one when debris was flying around, that you were her protection from the fire, explosions, and heat. When terror overwhelmed and safety vanished like a cloud, you were there. Thank you for the coincidences that you provided: the desk as shelter and the man's voice calling out a safe route. It was all you, Lord.

We're in awe of your goodness to us when so many others perished. We don't understand why you spared her life and others died. Surely some of them loved you, Lord, just as we do. Why was your right hand extended to us and not to them? God, we weep for those whose loved ones died. We feel guilty, somehow, that our family is still intact. Yet God, our whole family shouts praise for your rescue. You have delivered us from the hands of the wicked.

Thank you, Redeemer, that our loved one can watch her children grow up. Thank you for another chance to say, "I love you"; another chance to watch the blessings of each day unfold. Help us always give you praise for the miracle of this day.

"I will save you from the hands of the wicked and redeem you from the grasp of the cruel." (Jer. 15:21)

"Praise the LORD. Sing to the LORD a new song, his praise in the assembly of the saints." (Ps. 149:1)

A Mother's Prayer As Her Son Leaves for War

*L*ord, I say good-bye to my son today; this amazing adult who once lived inside my body. I remember the feel of him at my breast, the smell of shampooed hair, and the tiny hand reaching to my lips. Now he envelops me with strong arms for one last bear hug. Even as I struggle to smile so he won't feel torn, tears of grief and pride burst from me. He gently chides, but his tears mirror mine.

Will I ever see him again, God, this joy of my life, this one who loves you? If injury finds him, it won't be a scrape on his knee that Mommy can kiss and make better.

Help me not to fear, Lord. Help me not to worry. I raised him for you; help me open my hands and release him now. He belongs to you. He believes you for protection. Please protect him, God. He's depending on my prayers. Please beckon me to pray whenever he's in danger. I'll consider sleepless nights a gift—an extra opportunity to lift him to your throne.

Be the shield around him in strange lands. Give him the strength of steel under fire. Erase all fear with the power of your presence. Assure him of your ever-present love. Draw him closer to you and fill him to overflowing with your Holy Spirit. Make nobility and joy shine from him as a witness to others. And God, please bring him safely home, amen.

"Don't be intimidated by your enemies. This will be a sign to them that they are going to be destroyed, but that you are going to be saved, even by God himself." (Phil. 1:28 NLT)

Bless All Soldiers
Heading Off to War

O God, our strength and deliverer, we plead with you for the young men and women heading off to war. We love them all, Lord, even the ones we've never met. We love them for their willingness to travel to strange lands and fight in our place. We love them because they are your children and you love them. We love them because we are all part of the same human family and we empathize with their churning emotions.

Their youthful faces tug at our hearts, Father. We wish we could wipe away their loneliness, erase the heartache and guilt they feel for leaving loved ones behind, banish their dread of unknown lands, and dispel the danger. The only thing within our power, though, is to cry out to you on their behalf.

March into battle with them, Jehovah-Nissi—God our Banner. Be a shield around them. Protect their bodies from harm. Don't let the sights they see and the things they may be forced to do wound their hearts forever. Keep their spirits compassionate and loving in the midst of the turmoil around them. Lift them high on a cloud of your love, keeping them peaceful, calm, and close to you even though evil seems to prevail. Give them courage despite fear; honor in the face of temptation.

Live inside them, Lord, because they invite you. Let them recognize you as their commander, and if they die, welcome them home and say, "Well done, good and faithful servant." Amen.

"O LORD my God, I take refuge in you; save and deliver me from all who pursue me." (Ps. 7:1)

A Prayer for Our Troop Commanders

O God our deliverer, we kneel before you today on behalf of our military commanders—from the squad leaders to battalion commanders and the positions in all branches of the armed forces that correspond to those jobs. Responsibility weighs heavily on these men, Lord. They feel it in every waking moment; it prods them in nightmares. We thank you for the sense of duty that nags at them, Father, because it is incumbent on them to make certain our troops are prepared for war.

Give them wisdom and insight as they test each soldier. Compel these commanders to correct any deficiencies in their troops; push them to retrain any soldier they let slip under the standard. Make them insist that every soldier be up to task, because failing to properly teach one soldier could cost the lives of many soldiers. Teach them how to encourage each unit to work as one man, a team who will stand side by side to fight as brothers. Show them how to develop and maintain morale in their men.

Give each commander a fierce love for you, Lord. Help them to depend on you to supernaturally lead and protect. And then, when the real test comes on the battlefield, help them to turn all fear over to you, knowing their lives are in your hands, not the enemy's. We ask this in Jesus' name, amen.

"I lie down and sleep; I wake again, because the LORD *sustains me. I will not fear the tens of thousands drawn up against me on every side." (Ps. 3:5–6)*

Lord, Guide Our High-Ranking Military Leaders

O God our counselor, give wisdom and insight to every man and woman charged with preparing our country for war—from our Commander-in-Chief down through the one-star generals. Use them to accomplish your purpose—defeating those who stand against truth and justice. With your own hand, fit together the puzzle pieces of their war plan.

Open their ears to hear, Lord. Reveal when the time is right to move. Tell them when to strike and how to utilize our allies, making the troop movements flawless.

Open their minds, Lord. Make them flexible when unforeseen circumstances dictate a change in plan. Direct them to quickly implement new strategies. Help them catch any potential problems and move quickly to adjust their actions. Give them night vision in this dark time. Show them how to direct troops to encompass the enemy and then how to move in to cut off and destroy them. Give them courage to attack and not hold back.

Give them hearts that seek your face, holy God. Make them men of prayer. Comfort their souls through the agony they feel for the suffering of each individual soldier. We beg you, God, be the Commander of our commanders. Amen.

"'Because he loves me,' says the LORD, *'I will rescue him; I will protect him, for he acknowledges my name.'"* (Ps. 91:14)

Prayer for Needs in the News

O Lord, the news brings us close to people we will never meet in person—people in our nation and in countries all over the globe. We not only learn of their festivals and celebrations but also their troubles and the dangers they face—personal losses, natural disasters, wars, famine . . . so many tragedies. We watch with pain in our hearts and a sense of helplessness. There's so little we can do personally to allay their suffering, but we offer them the gift of our prayers.

Hear, O Lord, our prayer for the captured and imprisoned, for refugees who have been forced to flee their homelands, for those suffering the ravages of war, for those suffering hunger and disease, for those whose families have been torn apart, for those living in poverty, for those facing the challenges of illness or disability, for those grieving over the death of loved ones, for the powerlessness of the weak, and for the temptations and responsibilities of those in positions of leadership. Work your will in each heart and each situation. Break the power of evildoers. Meet the spiritual needs of those who seek after you.

Comfort and strengthen our Christian brothers and sisters, your ambassadors to this troubled world. As your representatives, may they reflect your image to those around them, whether in power or persecution. In all circumstances, turn hearts to you, God of love and ultimate ruler of all the nations. In the name of your Son, Jesus, who has secured for those who love him an eternity without tears, amen.

"We are therefore Christ's ambassadors, as though God were making his appeal through us. We implore you on Christ's behalf: Be reconciled to God." (2 Cor. 5:20)

Prayer Concerning the AIDS Epidemic

oly God, we bow before you in sorrow over this horrible mutating virus that threatens so many people around the world. It saddens us to see so much suffering, so many lives snuffed out in youth. Lord, protect all innocents from contracting this disease. We can't imagine how it must hurt you. You look down and see it all, and you desperately love every sufferer.

Lord, draw each of these people to you. Help them to face death squarely, realizing that they will soon meet their Creator. Show them clearly that if they have never repented of their sins, they will not go to heaven when they die. Then, if they have not asked for forgiveness, give them one last chance. Lead them to repentance, Father of mercy. Send friends or strangers who will guide them to accept you and make you Lord of their lives.

Send caregivers who will love them with your compassion. Mend any broken family relationships. Give them peace, ease their final hours, and welcome them home to heaven and everlasting life with you. In Jesus' name we pray, amen.

"Indeed, in our hearts we felt the sentence of death. But this happened that we might not rely on ourselves, but on God, who raises the dead." (2 Cor. 1:9)

Prayer for Persecuted Christians

*D*ear heavenly Father, we cry out to you today on behalf of our fellow Christians who are being persecuted around the world. Rescue them from the hand of their enemies. Renew their faith in you, even as their homes and churches are being destroyed. Give them a sense of your love amid their suffering and loss. Help them see your face and hear your voice.

Stretch out your hand of love and peace to all your children who have been imprisoned. Help them shine like lights in a dark place. May they feel your warm arms around them in the cold and lonely prison cells. Let these times of trials strengthen them, not destroy them.

Hear our prayers as we intercede for our persecuted brothers and sisters in Christ. We also lift up their families who struggle to live without them. We suffer when they suffer because we are all part of one body—the body of Christ. Remind us to pray for them often. We ask this in Jesus' name, amen.

"Remember those in prison as if you were their fellow prisoners, and those who are mistreated as if you yourselves were suffering." (Heb. 13:3)

Prayer When Nations Collapse

O God, no one in the entire world could have believed an enemy could do this to a great nation. The streets, which once bustled with people, languish in silence. Buildings that rose majestically, blotting out the sun, lie in rubble. Sagging flesh hangs from rotting bones and growling stomachs, but there is no food. The people weep through fear-filled, sleepless nights. Where can they turn, God? Who will help?

All the things they depended on are gone, Lord. Formerly lush fields now stretch endlessly as barren, mine-studded wasteland. Their homes crumble around these dear people; they can't recognize the wreckage where they once slept peacefully with their families. No one works; jobs evaporated with the crumbling economy. Wide, smooth roads undulate as chunks of concrete and asphalt—impassable. They writhe in pain, but there is no medicine and hospitals lie in ruins. The thin clothing they clutch around their bodies can't ward off the frigid winter. Help, Lord!

Lovers of false demon-gods hate the few Christians, Lord. They imprison and torture them. Your people cry until no more tears flow. Give them courage, God; see their anguish.

Lord, you remain the same through all generations. You don't abandon anyone forever. Come to the rescue! Have mercy, O God! Restore the nations and bring them to you. You are wonderfully good to everyone who seeks you. Turn hearts to wait for you, Lord. You are the only hope and help. Let all needy people trust in you. In Christ's name, amen.

"Yet I still dare to hope when I remember this: The unfailing love of the LORD never ends! By his mercies we have been kept from complete destruction. Great is his faithfulness; his mercies begin afresh each day." (Lam. 3:21–23 NLT)

A Prayer for the Innocent Victims in War Zones

O God of sorrows, you see and understand the plight of innocent women and children in war zones. Your heart aches for them, Father. You did not create pain; your enemy did. Your enemy chortles with glee when they suffer; you grieve.

This war is necessary to wipe out terrorism and defeat evil, yet these innocents did nothing to cause it. Perpetrators oppressed them long before the war began. And now bombs and land mines maim and kill them. They have nowhere to hide; terror surrounds them. You are their only hope, Lord. But they can't call out to you because most of them don't believe in you. They claim a false god as their protector. Reveal yourself to them, Lord.

Cup them in your hands and protect them. Hide them under your wings. Strengthen the dilapidated shelters over their heads with your strong arm. Breathe warmth on them when icy weather threatens; wrap them in your arms. Be the shield around them, God, and the comfort inside their hearts. Direct them when to flee and guide them to safety; send relief workers with food and medicine. We entrust these people to you, Lord, because we know you love them. There is no other God like you, amen.

"I am staggered by what I hear, I am bewildered by what I see. My heart falters, fear makes me tremble; the twilight I longed for has become a horror to me." (Isa. 21:3–4)

Keep me safe, O God, for in you I take refuge." (Ps. 16:1)

A Prayer of Help for the World's Refugees

*O*God of justice, how many years now have images of refugees flickered across our television screens? How many different tragedies have sent thousands upon thousands of homeless people streaming across barren, mine-infested lands? Trudging barefoot through the cold or stifling heat, starving, and separated from families and loved ones, they struggle for days or weeks, searching for safety and nourishment. It seems endless.

Our country sends food, Lord, huge bags of rice and flour. But since most is consumed by the oppressors, it offers little relief. We don't have the power to really change anything—but you do. So we ask you to do it, Lord. Let nourishing food and clean water get through to the refugees. Send workers who will tell them of your love.

Pour down your living waters and wash away the evil forces that cause so much pain in our world. Grant justice to the refugees. Help the people to call out to you in their affliction. Let your Holy Spirit flow into their hearts. Fill them with your peace that passes understanding. Comfort them in the midst of suffering. Be their refuge.

Ease their distress, Lord. Let them return safely home, taking you, their true refuge, along with them. In the name of Jesus, have mercy on the refugees, amen.

"Trust in him at all times, O people; pour out your hearts to him, for God is our refuge." (Ps. 62:8)

Strengthen Emergency Aid Workers around the World

*M*erciful Father, we kneel before you seeking strength for aid workers who help in emergency organizations around the world. We thank you for the love and compassion they hold out to people of many countries and races. They are your hands, Father, as they feed, clothe, and heal the victims of disasters. We thank you for their willingness to put their lives in peril as they selflessly give of themselves.

Protect them from the dangers of war; be an umbrella of safety when bombs fall and bullets fly. Guard their feet from hidden land mines. Watch over them through hurricanes, floods, and earthquakes.

Bless them, God. Grant them skill that extends well beyond formal learning. Refresh their bodies when work hours lengthen. Encourage them when the specter of human suffering seems too much to bear. Give them hope when there aren't enough workers or supplies or hours in the day. Keep them from guilt when the help they give isn't enough.

Help them to know when to reach out with a hug, Lord. And grant the workers who personally know Christ the privilege of sharing him with people who haven't met him. We pray in Jesus' name, amen.

Jesus said, "Therefore go and make disciples of all nations, baptizing them in the name of the Father and of the Son and of the Holy Spirit . . . And surely I will be with you always, to the very end of the age." (Matt. 28:19–20)

Contributors

Jeannie St. John Taylor (author and general editor), professional artist, conference speaker, wife, and mother of three has authored several books. *How to Be a Praying Mom*, from Hendrickson Publishers is her latest; *What Do You See When You See Me?*, a picture book from Cook Communications, is due out April 2002. Contact her on her web site: www.artwrite.org.

Petey Prater (major contributor), a Bible teacher and conference speaker, has led weekly prayer groups for thirty-five years. She has published poems, articles, and coauthored a devotional book. Married for forty-one years, she has four married children and three grandchildren.

Barbara Martin (major contributor) is coauthor of two children's devotional books, *What Would Jesus Do Today?* and *Walking with Jesus One Step At a Time*. She and her husband live in Portland, Oregon. She is currently working on a seven-book fantasy series.

Brian Burdon teaches junior high biology by day and Bible Study Fellowship classes by night in Seattle, Washington.

Sandy Cathcart is a freelance writer living in Prospect, Oregon. She directs the annual Oregon Christian Writers Conference in Salem, Oregon.

Marilyn Dale, a former flight attendant and nurse, currently uses her talents to minister to people as a nurse herbalist. She lives with her dog Nikki in Portland, Oregon.

Terri Eastburn considers her two girls and her husband her profession. She lives in the Northwest and has served the Lord for ten wonderful years. Terri is a native Oregonian.

Thomas E. Fuller, television reporter, writer, pastor, worship leader, and communications professional, lives in Newberg, Oregon and pastors Living Waters Christian Fellowship.

Judy Gann, children's librarian and freelance writer, lives in Lakewood, Washington. She is currently writing a devotional book for people with chronic illness.

Helen Haidle is an award-winning author of 35 children's books such as *He is Alive!* and *The Candymaker's Gift*. Look for her newest adult gift book of three Christmas legends, which will be published by Honor Books in the Fall of 2002.

Amy Haskins is a former social worker who now spends her time loving her foster children in the name of Jesus. She is married to Mike.

Mike Haskins has worked with troubled teens and been a youth pastor in San Diego, California and Portland, Oregon. He is married to Amy.

Dixie Lynn Johnson's gift of writing humor has transformed her tears into wheelbarrow loads of laughs. She lives in Oregon with husband, Bill, and two teenage sons.

Kathi Kingma lives with her policeman husband and their infant son in Molalla, Oregon. Her stories have appeared in collections.

Bette E. Nordberg lives in Puyallup, Washington with her husband and four kids. An accomplished musician and seamstress, she is the award-winning author of Serenity Bay and Pacific Hope, both published by Bethany House. Web address: www.myfables.com.

Cherie Norman, nurse, wife, and mother, works with drug addicts in Portland, Oregon. Her prayer is that those God puts in her path will achieve their highest potential in him.

Virginia Poulous has taught high school English and journalism, edited books, and written for a local newspaper. She just completed her first novel.

Betty Ritchie, a teacher by training, writes children's books and Sunday school curriculum. She and her husband, Pastor Bill Ritchie, live in Vancouver, Washington.

Nancy Billingsley Russell, a freelance writer and substitute teacher, lives on four and a half acres with her husband, three talented LD/ADD sons, and a hoard of critters.

Sharon C. Smith is a freelance writer from the state of Washington.

Susan Standley is a retired credit union CFO, a full-time "grammy," school volunteer, pray-er, and faithful friend.

Ray Taylor is a retired federal criminal investigator who juggles his time between an investigative agency and his small beef farm. He also coaches high school basketball.

Ron Taylor, a retired teacher and coach, teaches part-time in a local prison and leads prison Bible studies with Nancy, his wife of 36 years. He is the grandfather of Austin, Dylan, and Trevor.

Ty Taylor is a math class teaching assistant just completing his master's degree at Oregon State University in Corvallis, Oregon.

Glenn Thomas, father, grandfather and pray-er, was married to his wonderful wife for forty-nine years. He looks forward to seeing her again in heaven.

Index